WITHOUT A NET

WITHOUT A NET

The Female Experience of Growing Up Working Class

Edited by **Michelle Tea**

SEAL PRESS

"Another Year Older and Deeper in Debt" by Rachel Ann Brickner was originally published in *Scoundrel Time* literary journal in 2017: http://scoundreltime.com. "Steal Away" by Dorothy Allison was originally published in the collection *Trash*, published by Plume in 2002. Reprinted by permission of the author.

Seal Press
Hachette Book Group
1290 Avenue of the Americas, New York, NY 10104
sealpress.com
@SealPress

Printed in the United States of America
Published by Seal Press, an imprint of Perseus Books, LLC,
a subsidiary of Hachette Book Group, Inc. The Seal Press name and logo is a trademark of the Hachette Book Group.

Library of Congress Cataloging-in-Publication Data
Names: Tea, Michelle, editor.
Title: Without a net : the female experience of growing up working class / edited by Michelle Tea.
Description: Revised edition. | New York, NY : Seal Press, [2017]
Identifiers: LCCN 2017036031 (print) | LCCN 2017044694 (ebook) | ISBN 9781580056670 (ebook) | ISBN 9781580056663 (pbk.)
Subjects: LCSH: Working class women--United States.
Classification: LCC HD6095 (ebook) | LCC HD6095 .W63 2017 (print) | DDC 305.48/230973--dc23
LC record available at https://lccn.loc.gov/2017036031

LSC-C

10 9 8 7 6 5 4 3 2 1

CONTENTS

INTRODUCTION

MICHELLE TEA

I DIDN'T GROW UP POOR, IMPOVERISHED, DEPRIVED. *WE GOT BY.* WE HAD enough. And it's true—I had MTV and Catholic school. No college, though, but who went to college? Kennedys! My mom had money for Depeche Mode tickets when I begged her for them. Other times, no money for a candy bar. *Don't you think that if I had it I would give it to you?* Really, no money for a candy bar? Really.

We weren't broke, though. We were like everyone else in Chelsea, Massachusetts, and certainly better than many, the immigrant families crammed ten to an apartment, on welfare, or the families with a really bad alcoholic drinking all the money away. Our alcoholic dad split, no child support but that's O.K., my mom doesn't want to take nothing from nobody, no handouts, no charity. See? If we were *really* poor we'd need more. We'd be on food stamps, and we were only on them that one time when Ma had a hysterectomy and couldn't work. Ma had to take off her jewelry, the thin, gold chain she wore, laden with little golden charms, a Tweety bird, Nefertiti, *#1 Mom*. If the case worker saw the gold they might think she was rich. A single mother, a nurse, raising two children in a slummy town, a deadbeat father run out the door, she doesn't think we're poor, fears we could actually be mistaken for rich by the workers who grant us our food stamps. Such is the head fuck of class in America.

This book, *Without a Net*, is important because it actually acknowledges that class exists in America. It investigates the particular intersection of class and gender, and calls into the story additional intersectionalities that complicate and illuminate. In a country where a racist white electorate voted in a fascist billionaire as an answer to their economic woes, a book like this is a lightning bolt of sanity. In a country where everyone, rich and poor, claims to be middle class, denying the reality of class stratification even as it intensifies and the government wages a very clear class war, attacking the voting right, health care, and educational opportunities, this book is radical. It was a necessary book, truth-telling and fearless, when it was first published, and the addition of new voices in this fresh edition makes it even more relevant. The class problem, the problem of poverty and the strange way it is regarded in this country, is not going away, and we need writers from low-income backgrounds breaking through the *actual* middle-class, often rich viewpoints and experiences that dominate the media. We need to hear about the poor kid who grows up to pass as privileged among her peers. The poor kid who grows up, jumps a class or two, and sags with survivor's guilt every day. The anxious persistence of scarcity issues, the PTSD of a low-income childhood. The intersections of fat and poor, of brown or black and poor, of immigrant and poor. Radical, truth-telling magic. It might not be enough to rouse the country from its stupor of denial, ignorance, and hate, but at the very least it can be a lifeline thrown from one broke girl to another, and what a revelation it is to see your experience radiated back at you in a culture that denies you even exist.

The class problem, the problem of poverty and the strange way it is regarded in this country, is not going away.

I'm so grateful for the readers and teachers who have kept this book in print all these years. I'm grateful to share political community with the writers in this book, to be part of a sisterhood of broke girls. No matter if we grow up and manage to do alright for ourselves, the way history haunts our psyches, the way family can be left behind, it weighs on our hearts.

May this book make its way to a new generation of readers who need it, who learn from it and take solace in it, who use it to counter the lies our culture tells us and inspire their own stories.

ANOTHER YEAR OLDER AND DEEPER IN DEBT

RACHEL ANN BRICKNER

SAY I TELL YOU A STORY ABOUT A GIRL WHO'S AFRAID OF MONEY. FROM A young age, she learned that there didn't seem to be much of it and that hard work didn't mean one would ever have much of it. She knew this from her dad's dark tan in the summer that came from working twelve-hour days in the sun, laying mulch and planting flowers in the big, bright lawns of those with houses the size of her entire apartment complex. She knew this from her mom waking up early to go to an office job, and then going to work at an Italian restaurant rather than coming home, so that "after work" only meant the time it took her to get from the first job to the second one.

Say she asks for a pretend checkbook for her eighth birthday and makes her mom teach her how to balance it. She loves to practice her signature, the feeling of the thin paper on the side of her pinky as she writes. She loves to imagine buying things of her own someday—a bicycle, an old VW Bug, a small blue house—someday when she has more money than her parents.

By the time she's a teenager, she hasn't learned much more than this: Never let the balance go below zero. She spends the money from her baby-sitting jobs on thrift-store clothes, fast food, CDs. Later, she spends it on gas for her dad's truck when she borrows it to get to and from her after-school job. She works at a pizza shop now, with almost all older boys and men twice her age.

Say this girl starts out making only $5.25 an hour, and by the time she applies to college, her dad has left. She has only a couple hundred dollars to her name and relies on the men at work who like her to give her rides home. For a few dollars here and there, she burns CDs full of music for these men—metal and old rock, the kind of stuff that bores her—which she steals from the internet.

One of these men takes an interest in her. He's broad-shouldered with bright red hair and a kind smile. He's the one who will drive her home most often, late at night, when her mom has already gone to bed. Sometimes this girl goes on pizza deliveries with this man in his truck and they talk, joke, laugh. She feels seen by him more than by anyone else, and she thinks he might feel the same way. Sometimes, in the dark, in front of her parents' house, he looks at her for too long, then asks if he can give her a hug before she leaves him. She hesitates, then says yes. When he holds her, she feels comforted but also scared. She can feel he's getting something from this moment that she can't quite understand, and she's never completely sure if she's safe.

Eventually she pulls away from him, goes inside, takes a shower, and sleeps for less than a handful of hours before going to school.

She tells herself, *Everything is fine*. She tells herself, *I am safe*.

SAY SHE FINISHES HIGH SCHOOL WITH HONORS. SHE GETS TO wear a blue sash and silver cords around her neck at graduation, but her gown is wrinkled. She didn't realize she would have to iron it until it was too late and there was no one around to remind her. But on graduation day, both of her parents will come to the ceremony and watch their daughter receive her diploma, walking across the stage in bright teal flats, a huge smile across her face. After, they'll all go out to lunch, eating cheesecake silently in celebration, pretending to be the kind of family she wishes they could always be.

There will be no one to take her on visits to the colleges where her high school advisers told her to apply. So, she'll pick the school that's closest to home, only thirty minutes away. It's in the city, so she can get there on her own without a car. Besides, with small scholarships and grants, it's the cheapest option. The dorms, the campus, the classrooms are her escape plan.

Say some days this girl feels nothing but a bell jar of guilt around her head as she walks across the campus, although she's uncertain why. She thinks that maybe she doesn't belong here, in college, in these classes, with so many kids who seem unlike her with money to spend—on books, on beer, on tuition.

In every classroom, she sits close to the wall and stays quiet. She looks up all the words she doesn't know, when no one is paying attention: *ostensible, extrapolate, pernicious, renege. How does one "unpack" a thought?* she wonders. No one else seems to care.

When she realizes how much debt she's in,
she stares at her ledger for days in disbelief.
How could a sum go so far below zero?

Later, when she realizes how much debt she's in, she stares at her ledger for days in disbelief, wondering if she should drop out. How could a sum go so far below zero? So much debt in only two years, she can never pay it back with pizza shop money or old man CD money. She tells herself that there must be a job that will pay enough for her to live when she graduates in two more years. This is what everyone has told her, so she stays, her mom co-signing more loans each semester tuition rises, not knowing that later her daughter will have months where she's unable to afford groceries and rent, even with a "good" job, one that requires a college degree.

She thinks of the cold pizza dough in her hands. Of the long, secret hugs in that man's truck. And she learns to pretend to know and to have more than she does.

Tell me what you expect for her. Tell me how you think her story ends.

THE BURDEN OF ENOUGH

IJEOMA OLUO

THERE IS $10,000 IN MY BANK ACCOUNT RIGHT NOW. TO SOME PEOPLE, that is not very much money. To me, it's an amount just large enough to give me heartburn. I check my balance every few days, with as much anxiety as I used to check when the balance was $20 . . . or -$20. I take a deep breath, log on, close my eyes for a second, and then look. Yep. It's still there.

The number was larger for a brief period of time. The day that the second half of my book advance came in, I was checking my account to see if I had enough money to cover the coffee I was drinking. I saw the suddenly sizeable balance and thought I was going to have a panic attack in the coffee shop. I thought there had been a cruel joke. Perhaps someone had put money into my account on accident and it was going to be ripped out only to leave me overdrawn. I was a good three minutes into worst case scenarios before it occurred to me that it might be the money for the manuscript I'd just turned in. When my agent confirmed that yes, this little tidy sum was indeed my book money, I sat there in the coffee shop and said to myself, "Well, now what."

Growing up, there was never a question of what to do with extra money, because there was never any extra money. My mom worked the swing shift at an adult care facility. Back-breaking work that paid little above minimum wage. On that, she raised three kids. Money, or lack thereof, kept my mom up nights. It kept her sitting in the rocking chair on our apartment balcony crying at 3 a.m. while she tried writing numbers in different orders in the hopes that there would be a combination that would keep us fed and the lights on. Money was the reason why we couldn't go to birthday parties and couldn't go on field trips. Money was why we had no phone, why we ate ramen for weeks, why we had to use the hot water next door to shower. Money was why we only went to the ER, why we never went to the dentist, why we took out our own stitches. Money was what we searched couch cushions for, why we never opened our mail.

Money was never a future or a past. Money was never an opportunity. Money was always an emergency. So now, I have an amount of money that must signal a great emergency ahead and I'm just waiting for it to come.

In a fit of anxiety over the number, waiting there to be taken by disaster, I started giving it away. First to family, then friends. Then, when that was done and the number still scared me, I started giving money to strangers. I gave it away with a refusal to look at what I was doing, avoiding the math in my head. Eventually, even without looking at my balance, I knew I'd given more away than even someone trying to avoid money could excuse, so I had to stop. I paid bills and fixed my car and then I ran out of places to put the money. So now the money is just sitting there. Waiting.

The first half of the advance was much easier. I was behind on my mortgage and knew that even if I weren't behind, I wasn't bringing in enough writing work to actually cover my bills. It was a stress, but a stress I've always known. When my advance came in I immediately sunk it into the mountain of debts I'd accumulated in the year since I'd moved to full-time freelance writing. I paid four months ahead on my mortgage, knowing that things would still be tight, but I'd be able to breathe for a while.

But now things are different. Right now there is no emergency to come and lift this burden off of me. My income from writing and speaking has been growing steadily and has consistently been enough to cover my bills (late, because I am still afraid of bills, but still paid). My mortgage is current. I even paid taxes. I know that I'm supposed to put this money into savings or something, right? But how? How can you just leave money there? If I leave it there, something will happen to take it all away. If I leave it there I will lose my job, or my car will break down or my kids will get sick. I know how to handle all of those things without money—I have handled all of those things without money many times. But I don't know how to lose money. I've never had money to lose before.

It turns out that even when the bills are paid and it's been years since a call I answered was met with a voice saying "this is an attempt to collect a debt," the panic attack still comes whenever the screen on my phone says "unknown."

"Spend it! Spend it now on whatever you want because you will never get an opportunity to buy whatever you want ever again." That was the voice inside my head for a few weeks. But it turns out that even if you do buy whatever you want, when you've never had money, the list of "whatever" doesn't come to much. I bought some dresses and some makeup, and I got my kids some toys and sports stuff, and then I kind of ran out of ideas. In my lifetime of poverty I never really dreamed of things. I just dreamed of being able to answer a call from an unlisted number without having a panic attack. But it turns out that even when the bills are paid and it's been years since a call I answered was met with a voice saying "this is an attempt to collect a debt," the panic attack still comes whenever the screen on my phone says "unknown."

I am an intelligent, hardworking woman. I worked my ass off to put myself through college and build up my writing career. But I look at this bank balance, this $10,000 that would seem like nothing to so many, and I feel dumb. I feel like a giant child. I feel like a caricature of overblown irresponsibility on a daytime talk show. I don't know what to do. One of my first jobs ever was as a teller at a bank and I used to see these kids younger than my eighteen-year-old self come in and put $10,000 checks into their money-market accounts like it was no big deal, and now I'm thirty-six and I have this money and the thought of putting it in savings, or investing it, or putting it in a college fund for my kids—it breaks me out in hives. I know that there are important, grown-up things I could be putting this money to right now to help secure my family's future, but I don't know how to start. I feel broken and foolish, and still, the money just sits there.

I know that this is an opportunity to learn. To learn how to put money aside and watch it grow. To begin to get used to a feeling of financial safety. But I'm not ready yet. I cannot set down this burden of financial struggle because if I get used to moving without it, I won't be strong enough to carry it when it comes back, and it has never not come back. The burden of financial responsibility will just have to wait until I'm absolutely convinced that it's here to stay. I'm sure that doesn't make sense. I'm sure that someone who was raised to "set a little aside" each month is shaking their head at me in disgust. But when I was growing up, every time someone told my family to "set a little aside" each month it was an insult.

There are worse problems to have than trying to figure out how to not feel desperately poor when your bank account challenges the only reality you've ever known. My children are free from the bulk of that burden. Even in the tough times these last few years, they weren't the type of tough that had my kids showering next door or eating in soup kitchens. They go to birthday parties and go on field trips, and when they grow up they will probably not flinch at a call from an unlisted number and will open their mail the day it arrives. I worry that I haven't taught my children how to save money—I don't know how. But I figure that at least not being terrified of money is a head start that I never had.

I will figure out how to be responsible with this money somehow. Or I won't. No matter what, I'll be O.K., because I've always had to find a way to be O.K. But right now, I don't have to try to find a way to be O.K., because things just *are* O.K. I just have to try to find a way to appreciate that while it lasts.

STEAL AWAY

DOROTHY ALLISON

MY HANDS SHAKE WHEN I AM HUNGRY, AND I HAVE ALWAYS BEEN HUNGRY. Not for food—I have always had enough biscuit fat to last me. In college I got breakfast, lunch, and dinner with my dormitory fees, but my restless hunger didn't abate. It was having only four dollars till the end of the month and not enough coming in then. I sat at a lunch table with the girls who planned to go to the movies for the afternoon, and counting three dollars in worn bills the rest in coins over and over in my pocket. I couldn't go see any movies.

I went, instead, downtown to steal. I became what had always been expected of me—a thief. Dangerous, but careful. Wanting everything, I tamed my anger, smiling wide and innocently. With the help of that smile I stole toilet paper from the Burger King rest room, magazines from the lower shelves at 7-Eleven, and sardines from the deli—sliding those little cans down my jeans to where I had drawn the cuffs tight with rubber bands. I lined my pockets with plastic bags for a trip to the local Winn Dixie, where I could collect smoked oysters from the gourmet section and fresh grapes from the open bins of produce. From the hobby shop in the same shopping center I pocketed metal snaps to replace the rubber bands on my pantleg cuffs and metal guitar picks I could use to pry loose and switch price tags on items too big to carry away. Anything small enough to fit a palm walked out with me, anything round enough to fit an armpit, anything thin enough to carry between my belly and belt. The smallest, sharpest, most expensive items rested behind my teeth, behind that smile that remained my ultimate shield.

On the day that I was turned away from registration because my scholarship check was late, I dressed myself in my Sunday best and went downtown to the Hilton Hotel. There was a Methodist Outreach Convention with meetings in all the ballrooms, and a hospitality suite. I walked from room to room filling a JCPenney shopping bag with cut-glass ashtrays showing the Hilton logo and faceted wineglasses marked only with the dregs of grape juice. I dragged the bag out to St. Pete beach and sailed those ashtrays off the pier like frisbees. Then I waited for sunset to toss the wineglasses high enough to see the red and purple reflections as they flipped end over end. Each piece shattered ecstatically on the tar-black rocks under the pier, throwing up glass fragments into the spray. Sight and sound, it was better than a movie.

THE PRESIDENT OF THE COLLEGE INVITED ALL OF THE SCHOLARship students over for tea or wine. He served cheese that had to be cut from a great block with delicate little knives. I sipped wine, toothed cheese, talked politely, and used my smile. The president's wife nodded at me and put her pink fleshy hand on my shoulder. I put my own hand on hers and gave one short squeeze. She started but didn't back away, and I found myself giggling at her attempts to tell us all a funny story. She flushed and told us how happy she was to have us in her home. I smiled and told her how happy I was to have come, my jacket draped loosely over the wineglasses I had hooked in my belt. Walking back to the dorm, I slipped one hand into my pocket, carefully fingering two delicate little knives.

Junior year my scholarship was cut yet again, and I became nervous that working in the mailroom wouldn't pay for all I needed. St. Vincent de Paul offered me a ransom, paying a dime apiece for plates and trays carted off from the cafeteria. Glasses were only good for three cents and hard to carry down on the bus without breaking, but sheets from the alumni guest-room provided the necessary padding. My roommate complained that I made her nervous, always carrying boxes in and out. She moved out shortly after Christmas, and I chewed my nails trying to figure out how to carry her mattress down to St. Vincent de Paul. I finally decided it was hopeless, and spent the rest of the holidays reading Jean Genet and walking through the art department hallways.

They had hardwood stools in the studios, and stacking file boxes no one had opened in years. I wore a cloth cap when I took them, and my no-nonsense expression. I was so calm that one of the professors helped me clear paper off the third one. He was distracted, discussing Jackson Pollock with a very pale woman whose hands were marked with tusche. "Glad they finally decided to get these out of here," was all he said to me, never once looking up into my face. My anger came up from my stomach with an acid taste. I went back for his clipboard and papers, but his desk was locked and my file broke on the rim. In compensation I took the silk lining out of the pockets of the corduroy coat he'd left thrown over a stool. The silk made a lemongrass sachet I gave my mother for her birthday, and every time I saw him in that jacket I smiled.

MY SOCIOLOGY PROFESSOR HAD RED HAIR, FORTY SHELVES OF books, four children, and an entirely cordial relationship with her ex-husband. When she invited me to dinner, I did not understand what she wanted with me. I watched her closely and kept my hands in my pockets. She talked about her divorce and the politics in the department, how she had worked for John F. Kennedy in 1960 and demonstrated for civil rights in Little Rock in '65. There were lots of books she could lend me, she insisted, but didn't say exactly which ones. She poured me Harveys Bristol Cream, trailing her fingers across my wrist when I took the glass. Then she shook her head nervously and tried to persuade me to talk about myself, interrupting only to get me to switch topics as she moved restlessly from her rocking chair to her bolster to the couch beside me. She did not want to hear about my summers working in the mop factory, but she loved my lies about hitchhiking cross-country.

"Meet me for lunch on Monday," she insisted, while her eyes behind her glasses kept glancing at me, turning away and turning back. My palms were sweaty, but I nodded yes. At the door she stopped me, and put her hand out to touch my face.

"Your family is very poor, aren't they?"

My face froze and burned at the same time. "Not really," I told her, "not anymore." She nodded and smiled, and the heat in my face went down my body in waves.

I didn't want to go on Monday but made myself. Her secretary was confused when I asked about lunch. "I don't have anything written down about it," she said, without looking up at her calendar.

After class that afternoon the sociology professor explained her absence with a story about one of her children who had been bitten by a dog, but not seriously. "Come on Thursday," she insisted, but on Thursday neither she nor her secretary were there. I stood in the doorway to her office and tilted my head back to take in her shelves of books. I wanted to pocket them all, but at the same time I didn't want anything of hers. Trembling, I reached and pulled out the fattest book on the closest shelf. It was a hardbound edition of *Sadism at the Movies*, with a third of the pages underlined in red. It fit easily in my backpack, and I stopped in the Student Union bookstore on the way back to the dorm to buy a Hershey bar and steal a bright blue pen.

On the next Monday, she apologized again, and again invited me to go to lunch the next day. I skipped lunch but slipped in that afternoon to return her book, now full of my bright blue comments. In its spot on the shelf there was now a collection of the essays of Georges Bataille, still unmarked. By the time I returned it on Friday, heavy blue ink stains showed on the binding itself.

Eventually we did have lunch. She talked to me about how hard it was to be a woman alone in a college town, about how all the male professors treated her like a fool, and yet how hard she worked. I nodded.

"You read so much," I whispered.

"I keep up," she agreed with me.

"So do I," I smiled.

She looked nervous and changed the subject but let me walk her back to her office. On her desk, there was a new edition of Malinowski's *The Sexual Life of Savages*. I laid my notebook down on top of it, and took them both when I left. Malinowski was a fast read. I had that one back a day later. She was going through her date book looking for a free evening we could have dinner. But exams were coming up so soon. I smiled and nodded and backed out the door. The secretary, used to seeing me come and go, didn't even look up.

I TOOK NO OTHER MEALS WITH PROFESSORS, DIDN'T TRUST MYSELF in their houses. But I studied their words, gestures, jokes, and quarrels to see just how they were different from me. I limited my outrage to their office shelves, working my way through their books one at a time, carefully underlining my favorite passages in dark blue ink—occasionally covering over their own faded marks. I continued to take the sociology professor's classes but refused to stay after to talk, and when she called my name in the halls, I would just smile and keep walking. Once she sat beside me in a seminar and put her hand on the back of my neck where I was leaning back in my chair. I turned and saw she was biting her lips. I remembered her saying, "Your family is very poor, aren't they?" I kept my face expressionless and looked forward again. That was the afternoon I made myself a pair of harem pants out of the gauze curtains from the infirmary.

> I studied their words, gestures, jokes, and quarrels to see just how they were different from me.

MY PARENTS CAME FOR GRADUATION, MAMA TAKING THE DAY OFF from the diner, my father walking slow in his back brace. They both were bored at the lunch, uncomfortable and impatient to have the ceremony be over so we could pack my boxes in the car and leave. Mama kept pulling at the collar of my robe while waiting for the call for me to join my class. She was so nervous she kept rocking back on her heels and poked my statistics professor with her elbow as he tried to pass.

"Quite something, your daughter," he grinned as he shook my mama's hand. Mama and I could both tell he was uncomfortable, so she just nodded, not knowing what to say. "We're expecting great things of her," he added, and quickly joined the other professors on the platform, their eyes roaming over the parents headed for the elevated rows at the sides and back of the hall. I saw my sociology professor sharing a quick sip from the dean's pocket flask. She caught me watching, and her face flushed a dull reddish gray. I smiled widely as ever I had, and held that smile through the long slow ceremony that followed, the walk up to get my diploma, and the confused milling around that followed the moment when we were all supposed to throw our tassels over to the other side. Some of the students threw their mortarboards drunkenly into the air, but I tucked mine under my arm and found my parents before they had finished shaking the cramps out of their legs.

"Sure went on forever," Mama whispered, as we walked toward the exit.

The statistics professor was standing near the door telling a tall black woman, "Quite something, your son. We're expecting great things of him."

I laughed and tucked my diploma in Mama's bag for the walk back to the dormitory. People were packing station wagons, U-Haul trailers, and bulging little sedans. Our Pontiac was almost full and my face was starting to ache from smiling, but I made a quick trip down into the dormitory basement anyway. There was a vacuum cleaner and two wooden picture frames I'd stashed behind the laundry-room doors that I knew would fit perfectly in the Pontiac's trunk. Mama watched me carry them up but said nothing. Daddy only laughed and revved the engine while we swung past the auditorium. At the entrance to the campus I got them to pull over and look back at the scattered buildings. It was a rare moment, and for a change my hunger wasn't bothering me at all. But while my parents waited, I climbed out and pulled the commemorative roses off the welcome sign. I got back in the car and piled them into my mama's lap.

"Quite something, my daughter," she laughed, and hugged the flowers to her breast. She rocked in her seat as my stepfather gunned the engine and spun the tires pulling out. I grinned while she laughed.

"Quite something."

It was the best moment I'd had in four years.

FARM USE

JOY CASTRO

AFTER THE DIVORCE, MY MOTHER'S FIRST ENTREPRENEURIAL EFFORT FAILS. She opens a resale clothing shop and gives it a clever name: Encore. But in small-town West Virginia, people's used finery is a shabby thing. Her clientele has none of the chic-girl-down-on-her-luck wit the name deserves. Instead of Jean Rhys heroines, she attracts fat, bad-smelling women who slap their kids. There is nothing vintage to find. Her racks hold only the same clothes that once hung at Hill's and Heck's, the budget department stores. But they're dingier, with the smell of stale closets. At the counter, irritated women claim their things are worth more than my mother thinks.

Even in the black-and-white wedding photos, my mother's eyes have a touch of sleaze, a come-hither Joan Collins glint. My father's face is young, eager, shining; he looks toward her.

She looks at the camera, chin lowered, one white satin toe pointed forward, eyes leveling their invitation.

Once she and some other stewardesses partied on a yacht with O. J. Simpson, she tells me when I'm nine. I think how much fun it would be: throwing footballs on the deck, eating cake all day.

HIS HANDS ARE FURRED BLACK, HIS HEAD BALD AND SHINY, HIS gut a fat ball under graying T-shirts. He buys my brother Tonka trucks, buys me the radio I crave, buys my mother clothes and me a plum velvet blazer, very grown-up, for wearing to the Kingdom Hall. "Won't it be nice," my mother purrs, "to use the child support your father sends just on school clothes and nice things, instead of bills?"

She's got us there. I'm sick of food stamps and government cheese and clothes discarded by strangers. Middle school is a bad time to be poor. And I'm tall for my age and pretty. At assemblies, eighteen-year-old brothers from other congregations flirt with me between sessions, ask my mother if they can take me out. They back away, apologizing, when they learn I'm twelve. I want a black leather clutch purse and combs for my hair.

But not this way. I argue with her, but things move quickly. He makes fourteen dollars an hour working construction. He's a respected brother; he's served at Bethel. A date is set. I'm to wear my plum velvet blazer. My brother, seven, is to give her away in the ceremony at our Kingdom Hall.

"Won't that be cute?" she says.

"No, not really," I say.

I CRY IN HER ROOM AS SHE DRESSES, BEGGING HER NOT TO DO IT, not to do it, but I have no evidence aside from the weird way he looks at us. She's patient for a while, going over the money he makes, the good reputation he has in his congregation—but finally she turns on me.

"I am just about fed up, you hear? Do you understand me? I've just about had it with your bellyaching." She swings the hairbrush in my face. "Why do you always want to ruin everything? Why? One good thing comes along, something that will actually make me happy for once, and you have to start your whining. As usual."

"He's not a good man." I'm still crying. She laughs angrily, throws the brush down on the bureau.

"What do you know about good men? You're twelve years old." Her voice is rich with disgust. "Do you think you know what a good man is? Do you?" She shakes me. "Well?" I just cry. "Do you think your father's a good man?" I look at the brown and green carpet.

"Yes."

She stares at me, then lets me loose with a final shake and turns her back. She steps into the silky fawn dress.

"Well, that just shows what you know." It's early in the day, but the wide straps of her bra are already gouging into her shoulders, scoring the red welts we see when she changes into her nightgown at night. She tosses her head, talks to the mirror. "You listen here. I'm getting married today, and there's nothing, absolutely nothing, that you can do about it. Do you hear me?"

"Yes."

"For your information, young lady, I am happy. You can be happy, too, or you can sit in the corner and snivel. Is that clear?"

"Yes."

When the elder asks, "Who gives this woman in marriage?" my brother, confused, must be prodded to speak. "I do," he says, worried, his eyes casting about to see if he's done the right thing.

The promised wealth does not materialize. Our stepfather visits numerous doctors until one agrees to sign the papers that say he has black lung. He has bullied our mother into selling her share of the store, into selling our house, into buying a trailer and moving hours away to a trailer park in a small town where we know no one.

We start the new school shabby, in castoffs. If we want clothes for school, my stepfather tells us, we can have a yard sale, sell our toys. Our mother urges us to comply; we'll feel so much better if we have some nice things.

The first disability check arrives. He stops working, stays home. He's constantly there, watching.

The money problems worsen. Our clothes are not replaced. We start the new school shabby, in castoffs. If we want clothes for school, he tells us, we can have a yard sale, sell our toys. Our mother urges us to comply; we'll feel so much better if we have some nice things.

All Saturday we sit in the yard. Strange kids pick up my horse models, my brother's Matchbox cars and Tonka trucks. One by one the items go, my plastic family of smoke-gray Arabians scattered.

We make almost a hundred dollars. It can buy new shoes for both of us, new pants for my brother, maybe a sweater for me.

My stepfather takes the stacks of ones. There will be no clothes. Everything that's ours, he says, is his. Get used to it.

We go to school ragged, mismatched, hopeless.

IN RURAL AREAS, THE OCCASIONAL TRUCK HAS FARM USE PAINTED on its sides, a special dispensation to relieve the family farm of the expenses of a license, insurance.

In the back, sometimes, gaunt children ride, their arms wrapped tiredly around their knees, hunched amid bales or firewood or piles of scrap. They stare dead-eyed into the car behind.

My brother and I are those children. Our arms are wrapped around our knees. Our stepfather drives our Farm Use truck all over town: to the post office, the grocery. We sit in the back, staring at children belted safely into seats beside their parents. Sometimes, they're children from school, children we know.

They point, talk to their parents excitedly, stare at us in fascination and disgust.

My ass is a moving target. I cannot pass the couch without a slap, a pinch, a long stroke that ends in squeezing. I walk as quickly, straightly, as invisibly as I can. "This girl of yours sure does love to wiggle, don't she, Mother?" he calls to the kitchen.

"Yes, she does," comes a deadened voice.

As time passes, the rules intensify. Work is a punishment; after school, we clear brush until we cannot see to sickle. We carry wood. Dig ditches for the gas lines. Food becomes a measured thing. Each mealtime, my stepfather dishes himself up from the pots. Then my mother may help herself to half of what he has taken. Then, while he watches, she can spoon half of what she's taken onto my plate. A portion half the size of mine goes to my brother. If my stepfather wants one peanut butter and jelly sandwich, my brother gets one-eighth. If she gives us more than my stepfather calculates is correct, he beats us with his belt.

We sit at dinner, our eyes on our plates. If we look our stepfather in the eye, ever, without being told to, we're beaten.

"How those little titties of yours doing?" he says to me. "They must be sprouting pretty good right about now."

If I do not keep eating, I'll have stomach pains later, or I'll have to eat dry the packets of Carnation Instant Breakfast we all get free in gym and which the other girls leave lying in their lockers.

After class, I try to make my voice casual. "Are you going to eat that?" I say, pointing.

They look at each other, grinning. Then back at me, their eyes cool and repelled. "No. My god. Take it if you want it."

You're supposed to pour it in milk, but I have no milk. On the school bus, I sink down so no one can see me and rip the top back, pour the dry grains in my mouth, chew. I learn to like it.

"Must be like two puppies. Isn't that right, Mother?"

"Yes."

"Two puppies with brown noses."

Something in my throat is clogging, but I chew, eyes down, head down. My brother keeps eating. I feel my mother's gaze like a beam of heat in my hair.

DOING DISHES, I PALM A STEAK KNIFE FROM THE KITCHEN, EASING the drawer silently open, sliding it into my pocket. In bed, I slide it under the side pillow, practice grabbing it in the dark, my hand darting to catch its handle fast as a rabbit's dash.

He finds it, lying beside me in the darkness as he has begun to do, breathing, his whole body stiff and heavy in the bed next to me. First, on top of the bedspread. Now under the sheets.

I think of nothing. I do not pray. I lie there in a stillness so extreme I might be dead, each nerve a wire humming with still terror.

"What's this?" he says. He sits up. "Turn that light on." I do. The room jumps to brightness, and I pull my arm back to my side. Only my eyes swerve to see the knife gripped in his hand.

"What you got this for, girly?"

I look at the window, the door, long for my mother to appear. "It's so isolated here. I get afraid. Of robbers, I mean." My voice is strangled, unbelievable.

"Is that so?" His grin leaks slowly across his mouth. It's a good game, cat and mouse. "Robbers."

"Yes. It's isolated here," I say.

"Well, no robbers are gonna get you. I'm here. I'm here to protect my little girl. You don't need this." He rises and moves around the bed to stand above me. "We don't want you cutting yourself by accident, do we? A sharp knife like this?" He holds the blade in my face. I push my head back into the pillow.

"No, sir," I whisper.

"Then I'll just take this back to the kitchen." Quick as a fox, his free hand reaches out and flips back the blankets, unzips my quilted pink nightgown, sternum to crotch, flips the fabric open. He stares down at me, my breasts, my hipbones, my white underwear. His eyes glitter. He grins down for a minute.

"So cover yourself up," he says. My hands fly to my waist, but the zipper snags, sticks, jerks upward. "Don't be so modest," he laughs. "Fathers have a right to see their daughters. It's natural." The corners of the room are thick with shadow. "And what am I?"

"My spiritual father," I whisper. I am a wax doll, empty, pliant, a cunning image of the girl who used to live here.

"That's right." The lamp clicks. The darkness becomes deeper darkness. "No more knives. You hear?"

"Yes, sir."

His steps shake the trailer as he moves down the hall.

THE WAY TO MAKE MY STEPFATHER A PIE IS THIS. FIRST, YOU MAKE the crust, the light, flaking, curling crust he requires every day. My mother does this with her family recipe and sets it aside. I meet her at the table in the yard, each of us holding a small knife.

Then you peel the apples—the small, sweet ones, the kind he likes, I don't know their names, I'm not allowed in the grocery store—and then you cut them in half, top to bottom, straight through the center. Then you cut the halves in half. Then you scoop the core out with the knife, following the lines in the apple's pale meat. Then you slice the cored quarters.

The slices will go into the crust, the dish will go into the oven, two pieces, hot, will go into their bowls, and his will get a scoop of Breyer's vanilla ice cream. Many times he tells us it's the best ice cream, as BMW is the best motorbike and Nikon is the best camera. Both of which he has. "Bavarian Motor Works," he likes to bellow, apropos of nothing.

My brother and I do not eat pie. It is a punishment. "Five desserts!" our stepfather yells when we err, leaping triumphantly to his feet to make the little marks, /////, on the sheet pinned to the wall for that purpose. When I run away, I am up to minus seventy-six desserts. We never get to zero. When we get close, he's more watchful. He loves to let us get to two or three.

It's fall. He's inside watching television. My mother and I sit in the yard, peeling, coring, slicing. The glossy apples disappear under our knives, emerge as neat pale slivers lying flat in the dish. I feel the slight resistance of the flesh, then the final quick *thunk* as blade hits board.

"I don't know what I'm going to do," she says in a low smothered voice.

I carve a red curling spiral away from the flesh. She glances at me, sighs noisily. "I just don't know what I'm going to do."

"What about?"

"About him."

I think she's going to talk about running again. I'm sick of running, sick of waking up in the motel bed to hear her whispering into the phone, promising, apologizing, giving him directions. I'm sick of the pains in my stomach when we head back east again. Maybe she's starting to plan, I think. But we have no car to run in now. He sold it after the last time. We're ten miles outside a little town in rural West Virginia. We know no one but Witnesses.

And we've been through that, spent nights at elders' houses, the blood drying on her lip, her eye blacked, my brother bruised and shaking, the two of us huddled silent on a strange couch. They send us home. It's a family situation, a private matter. They acknowledge the rule my stepfather holds over her like a swinging blade: Except in cases of adultery, a wife cannot divorce her husband. It's a sin. We go back.

But leaving isn't on her mind.

"I don't know what it's going to take." My quarters fall into clean fans of slices, which I gather and drop in the dish.

"What what's going to take?"

"What it's going to take to satisfy him."

My knife steadies itself against the board. "Meaning what?"

"He's never satisfied." Her voice drops to a whisper. "Nothing I do." She pushes a long lock of gray back from her face. All the curl's fallen out of it since he's made her grow it out. "Three, four times a day he wants it."

I cut my last apple through its center.

"You're a big girl. You know what I mean."

The halves into halves. The half-moons of the cores, the pith and seeds into the pot of waste.

"I could lose my mind," she says, her voice breaking. I stop cutting and look up. She's crying, but her hands don't stop moving. I can hear the creek. My brother is scything weeds in the distance. "I think it might kill me or something." She keeps her eyes on her apple, her knife. The trees rise dark up the mountain behind her. "He needs some other kind of—some kind of outlet." The only sound is her knife hitting the board as the slices separate.

I stare at her, at the wide dark bowl of the valley we live in. She glances up at me, then at the dish of apples.

"Here, have one," she says, fishing out a slice. Even though apples have been forbidden to my brother and me for months, I can remember their taste, their sour springing juice. She shakes it at me anxiously, glances at the trailer windows. For him to see this would mean a beating—for me, at least, if not for her.

"I think I'm done," I say, and stand up.

THE BEST PROFESSIONALS HAVE NEVER SEEN AN ARREST

NAOMI BEGG

WHEN I WAS FIFTEEN, I USED TO INVITE MY FRIENDS TO MY HOUSE ON THE weekends so we could watch people get arrested. Every Saturday, we'd gather around my living room window with snacks and maybe the TV on low in the background, and wait for something to kick off. When we heard the sirens coming up the hill to my street, we'd guess which kind of police vehicle it was: the car, the small van, the big van with the cages in the back. My mom was such an expert she had a one hundred percent success rate at guess-the-police-car. But she'd been playing since long before us.

If my friends and I were lucky it was the big van—like the time my neighbors took too much drugs and the only way the police could get them in the back of the van was to handcuff both their wrists *and* ankles and drag them out of their apartment block. Other times, like on small-car evenings, things would be less exciting, although somehow more memorable.

Like when the man across the street didn't take his medication and began running around the street in nothing but his tighty whities, in the rain, shouting "God is the cure for cancer!" It seemed strange he got arrested for that.

Naturally, after some time, my friends' parents found out what was happening and my friends weren't allowed to come over anymore. *Certainly* not on a weekend. Rather than being upset, I was amused. I thought my friends' parents were weak, and sheltered. *Those children will never get anywhere,* I thought to myself, *if they can't even handle a few drunk arrests.*

Fast forward a decade-and-a-bit, and all those same friends enjoy much more success than me. One is a train driver—a job which has very little social status but, I have discovered, an excellent salary and benefits. One studied law and is now a police officer—we don't speak anymore but I can only assume our weekend vigils in my living room window played a part in that decision. I have friends in project management, scientific research, website administration. They all earn more than me, have bought or could buy houses, drive nicer cars, go on more vacations, and generally have a much higher standard of living.

My friends were not smarter than me. All of us were among the top students in our year group. They weren't, at least as far as I can remember, more sociable or more likeable or more capable—again, we were all about the same caliber, give or take. We all went to reputable universities, got good degrees, and did internships and volunteer work in our chosen fields.

And yet.

And yet, I moved back in with my mom "temporarily" two years ago to save money and I still work part-time jobs to pay my bills. I teach at my local college, but it's not quite a full-time position, so I also have a retail job at a convenience store, selling milk, cigarettes, vodka, energy drinks. This is the same shop I worked in as a teenager, during the time my friends and I used to watch arrests out the window. I recently acquired my first car—unfortunately, it's twelve years old and even though I've only had it a few months I've already had to replace the battery twice.

I'm not unhappy, not really, but it's taking me much longer to get myself "sorted," whatever that means, than seems fair.

As it turns out, there is very little use in the professional world for the sorts of skills I was brought up to need: an instinct for when a fight is about to break out, no fear of wild-eyed addicts, the ability to seem friendly enough that you're not a snob (that'll get you a kicking) but not so friendly that you're a friend (that will also lead to a kicking). Meanwhile, since becoming a lecturer a year or so ago, I have discovered an inability to complete all sorts of tasks: calling colleagues (how should I introduce myself?), asking for help, using certain kinds of software, asking for help, sharing ideas, saying "no" to extra work, and asking for help.

I am ill-equipped for professional life. I always knew it would be the case, and as a student I applied for thousands of "admin" and "business" jobs, placements, and volunteer opportunities so I could learn, improve. In all cases I was rejected because I had zero prior experience, and in an overcrowded market where the other applicants could do the job in their sleep, why would anyone want to spend the time training me?

So, I continued in retail and bar work, did some mentoring, some tutoring, and some baby sitting. Not with the aim of becoming more "employable," or developing my skills, but out of sheer necessity. Life is expensive, and the kind of work I did, both as a student and a new graduate, was poorly paid. I *had* to hustle just to stay alive, there was no one else to support me. Occasionally, I would call my dad, a carpenter who fits windows and doors, and who could be counted on to rustle up enough money to replace my broken laptop or pay for the last week of groceries before payday. In that sense, I have been more privileged than others—even that is not possible for too many. And of course, as I mentioned earlier, I now live with my mom, which has given me a huge leg up financially.

I still spend a lot of time treading water, though. In hindsight, it was through doing all that hustling that I began to develop some of the skills I might need, but it was happening too slowly on a much too small scale. I could manage myself but I couldn't manage others—that would come to hold me back later. I could make conversation with any kind of person under the sun, but I wasn't confident in seeking out new information. I couldn't—in fact I still can't—negotiate or persuade, and they were skills I didn't even know existed. I had thought myself tough, brave, insightful, but I was professionally naive. I moved from one year to the next—twenty-four, twenty-five, twenty-six years old—adding each day to the list of things I didn't know or couldn't do, and all the while, Professional Life became a scarier and scarier prospect.

There is an odd sort of psychological catch-22 that happens when you straddle both worlds, the working-class world and the professional world: You realize you want success but you don't want to be a successful person.

I manage—nothing disastrous has happened yet, but it's hard. I keep a work journal of successes and failures and I am trying to force myself to ask for help more often. I live in permanent fear that today is the day, this is the class, here is the moment, when my cluelessness will be exposed. I am convinced my recent lucky streak—decent job, decent salary, a little discretionary spending money—is time sensitive. That's why I still stack shelves as a back-up—a girl can't be too careful.

It seems I am on the up. But there is an odd sort of psychological catch-22 that happens when you straddle both worlds—the working-class world of the shop and the professional world of the college. You realize you want success but you don't want to be a successful person. Straddling the line is impossible. I was always so proud of not being one of those people who needed a fancy job or fancy clothes to feel valuable. "Look at me!" I'd think. "I'm confident and happy and I stack shelves for a living while being unable to afford a car. That's real confidence!" I laughed at my "sheltered friends" who were banned from mixing with my neighbors, the "undesirables." I based my identity on being the kind of person who wasn't afraid to get her hands dirty, and didn't need to feel a sense of superiority over others in order to feel worthy. I refused to see that there were things I could learn from my more successful peers.

There is a link between how much we get paid and how valuable we feel, and so to earn both a little and a lot at the same time leaves you wondering which one is your "real" value. Logically, you know it's the higher one—if you weren't worth it then you wouldn't be earning it. But then what does that say about my "working-class" friends, my colleagues at the shop? Am I somehow worth more than them?

The conundrum is limiting because it fosters a negative attitude toward "success" (decent salary, breathing room in the budget) that I can't disengage from. More simply, I want success but I don't want to be a successful person. I want the management skills of my college colleagues, and I want their salary and lifestyle, but I never laugh with the other lecturers in the same way as I do with my shop colleagues. I have friends who work in bars and shops and have no money and I feel more at home with them than anyone else in the world. At times it occurs to me that perhaps I'm just romanticizing my "working-class roots" (a phrase I hate almost as much as "real, salt of the earth people") because I'm scared to take another step up the ladder. But if I give up this mentality, what is there to replace it? I won't ever be a Professional from a Professional family, but I have few role models of the Professional from an

Unprofessional family. It seems, as with everything else in life, we have to make it up as we go along.

So I no longer live in a house where I can see people being arrested on a weekly basis. I have friends now who have never, not once in all their lives, seen someone be arrested. I'm not convinced that's a good thing, but it does seem to be a very good thing professionally. And now that I have seen it, and can never unsee it, I will have to find a way to work around it.

THE PRISON WE CALLED HOME

SIOBHAN BROOKS

I WAS BORN IN THE SUNNYDALE HOUSING PROJECTS IN SAN FRANCISCO ON July 14, 1972. My mother had been living in the Haight Ashbury district, where she used to take pictures of the Bay Bridge from her apartment, but the rents increased and white people moved in, so she had to move. Being a single Black woman without a high school diploma, the projects were the only place she could find to live. And Sunnydale, known for its violence, always had vacancies.

These projects are the largest in San Francisco. Built during World War II, they look like red-and-white row houses. Though they are now predominantly Black (along with a few Asian, Latino, and Samoan families), they weren't always. White people used to live in them during the 1940s, when they functioned as military housing. Then the suburbs were built up, and white people went to live in those communities, keeping Blacks out, locked in the ghetto. It was strange for me to see old photos of Sunnydale with suburban-looking white families living there. The only white people who lived in Sunnydale when I was growing up were white women who mothered Black children and had been rejected from the white world.

Like most projects, Sunnydale had a reputation for violence, and was referred to as "Swampy Desert" or "Swampy D." My mother tried her best to make our unit seem like home. She bought beads, curtains, a birdbath, and marble tables that she ordered from catalogues in order to make the house look nice, in spite of the roaches that lived in the corner of our stove. We covered our food with foil to keep them away. I used to love watching her decorate our place with contact paper, woodprints, plants, and bright fabric that she would sew onto our chairs. She bought the initials A and S (for Aldean and Siobhan) to place outside our door.

I felt most loved by my mother at Christmas, when she would buy me dozens of gifts—toys, dolls, games, and clothes: Christmas was her way of proving that we weren't poor, even though we lived in the projects. One Christmas she bought a gingerbread house and wrapped it up to surprise me. I was delighted. I had never had a gingerbread house. While we were looking at the frosting and the smiling gingerbread man, I noticed some-thing brown on top of the house, moving. I pointed it out to my mother—it was a roach. My mother threw the gingerbread house across the room, then grabbed a hammer and crushed it to pieces. She said every racial slur toward Black people imaginable—because of her internalized racism, she often blamed her problems on being Black, not on the effects of white racism against us.

Once we were returning home from the circus and there was a horrible car accident. A little girl, also returning from the circus with her parents, got hit by a car and was killed. The driver was drunk, and the car had actually run through a liquor store; the girl was decapitated. As we approached the crowd, my mother, seeing something, led us in a different direction. We heard about the accident later on the news, and a Malcolm X mural was painted where the accident occurred, but there was no discussion as to why there were so many liquor stores in our area.

Another time there was a Black man running from unit to unit in Sunnydale breaking windows. He had been stabbed and wanted someone to call for help. My mother and I were relieved that he didn't break ours. We had bars on our windows to keep people from breaking in, but they also kept us locked in—if there had been a fire, they would have prevented our escape. Even so, we had our place broken into twice, both times through the door.

WHILE THESE EVENTS DIDN'T HAPPEN EVERY DAY IN THE PROJECTS, they are reflective of what it is like to grow up in them. Whether you're talking about projects in Los Angeles, San Francisco, Oakland, New Jersey, Philadelphia, New York, or Chicago, they all share the same incarcerating elements. While projects do have elements of culture, community, and resistance, they also have fear, sadness, hopelessness, and dramatically violent events that, no matter how infrequent, stay imprinted in the mind. There is limited access to space, a dearth of businesses, and intense social isolation. I remember riding the bus with my mother and passing banks, schools, and real-estate agencies, not realizing what they were. Most people in the projects carried cash and/or cashed their checks at a check-cashing place. Few people I knew had bank accounts.

The real-estate agencies were partly responsible for why Black people and other people of color could not live in safe housing. They often catered to the white elite, and steered people of color to the houses with the lowest property values. Poor people of color are forced to live in projects. For us, to be working class would have been a step up. We were the prelude to the working class, locked in a ghetto.

Growing up, we didn't have a playground. We went roof-hopping, played hide-and-go-seek in vacant apartment buildings, climbed trees. We tore the boards from the doorways of vacant units and rode them down nearby steps. We ate dirt, pulled sour grass and chewed on it. Later we were told it was called "sour grass" because the dogs peed on it.

Getting Exposure

The first time I entered a real house, I was eleven years old. I had a Filipina friend named Mary who lived a few blocks away, in one of the houses alongside Sunnydale populated mostly by Asians. Mary went to my elementary school; we were in the same third-grade class. I didn't know her well, but I noticed that she would walk the same way as me when my mother picked me up from school and disappear into one of those houses. One day she invited me over, out of the blue, and without asking my mother if it was O.K., I went.

I remember being amazed at how much space Mary and her family had, compared to the one-bedroom unit with the six-foot ceiling my mother and I shared; Mary's house was like a mansion compared to any unit in Sunnydale. They had a garage, four bedrooms (each of her siblings had their own room), a spacious bathroom, a kitchen with tile floors (clean, no roaches), and a living room with a fireplace. I had never seen a house like that except on television. I remember feeling very small in her house. Her mother was sweet, but wary of me in the beginning, watching my every move. Like many immigrants, she had been taught to fear Black people, and I was the first Black person they had ever had in their house. Even though they lived only a few blocks away from us, we lived in different worlds.

Growing up in the projects, it was common for us to refer to where we lived as our "house." My friends would always ask if they could come over to my house, and vice versa; we never said, "Can I come over to your unit?" But after visiting Mary in a real house, I felt how marginal we were in the projects. Things they took for granted, like space, were new to me. Mary's windows opened up to the view of a garden in the back, birds, and blue sky, without bars.

That day Mary's mother made us Rice Krispies Treats, and we played in her garage. It changed my life forever. After being in their house I never wanted to go back to Sunnydale. I continued to visit after school for an hour and play, becoming exposed to a whole new world. Living in the projects is very similar to living on a Native American reservation—the projects are located on poorly kept land, isolated from the rest of society, and controlled by the government. I recently read that HUD builds the houses on reservations as well as in the projects.

For people living in projects, all roads lead to the ghetto. Our whole social world usually does not expand far from it. The schools we attend are often near our neighborhoods, and, because of our lack of property-value-generated revenue, they have poor funding and overcrowded classrooms. Everyone I knew from school lived in a ghetto or not far from one. I hardly ever met middle-class people—Black, Latino/a, Asian, or white. At school we learned more about our social status by the lack of care the teachers gave us. I remember a class where the social sciences teacher just up and left class because he was tired of dealing with us. He was Black, and so were most of the students. During lunch we were not allowed to leave the campus, and we even had security guards standing outside the entrance. Sometimes the principal would use a lock and chain to keep us in. This was during a peak of gang activity in California, and the principal thought it was safer for us to stay inside during lunch. Once I cut class to visit a friend of mine at another school, which was mostly white; I was surprised by the amount of freedom they had. During lunch the students could sit outside on the grass, or leave the campus entirely.

Everywhere we went there was a police presence: school dances, the bus stop, a police helicopter flying over us at night. And we were always crowded into small spaces: the projects, the welfare lines, the bus. We never experienced the larger, open places in San Francisco. With inferior school systems and housing, the projects were often a prelude to the final form of incarceration: jail and prison. A few of the guys I grew up with ended up in jail, on probation, or dead, while the girls ended up single parents on welfare.

> If you want to succeed, all you need to do is act right, I believed. I didn't understand, at age fourteen, that our oppression had nothing to do with good behavior and everything to do with racism and classism.

Planning My Escape

The older I got, the more I hated Sunnydale and all communities of color like it. This is contradictory to the notion of being "down" with the ghetto, which some confused Black middle- and working-class people glorify and romanticize (often in gangsta rap and narrow Black nationalist ideology)—usually out of some strange guilt at being spared the "Black" experience of growing up in poverty. Living in an anti-Black, self-hating household, it was easy for me to begin to hate where I came from and the people we lived among. Contrary to the popular belief that people live in the projects because they are not ambitious, or because they are too lazy to get out, my mother had very bourgeois values and manners, which I shared. I had already decided that I was not going to live in the projects when I got older, or be like the people who lived there: If you want to succeed, all you need to do is act right, I believed. I didn't understand, at age fourteen, that our oppression had nothing to do with good behavior and everything to do with structural racism and classism.

During my high school years, my mother spared me household chores so that I could focus on my schoolwork, reading, and writing. I was allowed to be selfish in a way most of my friends were not, and in this regard I had more in common with my white friends than my friends of color.

Growing up in a nonworking environment, I had no working-class identity, and actually began to look down on people who were "just workers." I was going to be a thinker, a writer. When I was sixteen I got my first summer job working at the Presidio hospital doing clerical work, and was surprised when my paycheck did not fall on the first or fifteenth of the month, the dates welfare checks came.

I was fed up with the projects, and desperately wanted out. I hated living in fear of my neighbors, in fear of the men when coming home late at night, fearing the sound of helicopters. I hated being so far removed from the central areas of San Francisco. It took me an hour on the bus to get downtown. Cabs would refuse to bring me all the way home, letting me off where the homes ended and Sunnydale began. I decided that I would explore San Francisco on my own and slowly move out of the projects.

Once, when I was sixteen, I rode the buses until I was lost. I knew that I had to learn the city better if I were going to move outside of my racially segregated environment. I got off at a random stop and went into a cafe to get something to drink.

When I opened the door I was surprised and a bit frightened by what I saw: mostly white people eating and drinking coffee. Prior to opening the door I had never been in a predominantly white environment; I had actually only seen white people on television. I remember feeling awkward, looking at the white boy with piercings behind the counter and at the menu of drinks I couldn't pronounce. If I could successfully order a drink in this place, I thought, I could function outside of Sunnydale, since anything outside of Sunnydale was most likely to be white. I slowly walked up to the counter and mumbled that I wanted a cafe au lait, hoping I pronounced it right. He turned about and made my drink. I decided to drink inside the cafe and observe my surroundings. Most of my neighbors would have felt inferior or scared, and so they stayed where they were most comfortable and accepted—the ghetto.

I was reminded of how Blacks in my area feared white people, even though they would never admit it. I went to a Nirvana concert in the early nineties, at a venue near Sunnydale, the Cow Palace. I remember thinking that it was one of the rare times something was actually near us—usually we had to go far from our neighborhood to see a show or access services. Old Black men normally hung in front of neighborhood liquor stores until the wee hours of the morning, but on the evening of the Nirvana concert, mobs of white kids from the suburbs dominated their turf. Instead of the Black men being at their usual spots, these teenage white boys had taken it. It was the first time I actually wanted to see those Black men in front of the liquor store, claiming their space in the face of whiteness.

Escape from the Swamp

I moved out of the projects during my junior year at San Francisco State University, at the age of twenty-two. My longtime friend Jennifer, a white girl from a working-class background, became my housing hook-up. This is usually how people of color avoid racism and find housing. She used to live with a friend of ours near Golden Gate Park, and when she moved out she gave me her room. The rent was only two hundred dollars, but I remember thinking it was a lot of money to save each month. My mother only paid $160 for our unit in the projects, and she was getting government aid. I was scared to move, but took the challenge.

The day I moved out my mother was hurt; though she wanted me to succeed, she didn't want me to leave her. Once she'd even asked me if I was going to get a unit next door. I remember rolling my eyes and sighing, I'd rather die than live here another day. No one really moved out of Sunnydale, which is why my leaving was such a big deal. Most people move within Sunnydale, or to another housing project. I was doing something most people in Sunnydale could only dream of doing: moving into a nice, safe neighborhood outside of the projects.

LATER I MOVED INTO ANOTHER AREA, ALSO THROUGH JENNIFER, and lived with a white woman named Mary. While the (mainly white) people that I met in this new-world college neighborhood were nice to me, it was obvious to me that they didn't know many people of color, and the ones they did know were the very best of the best, the cream of the crop—not the average person of color. I call this the Super Nigger Syndrome—in order for a Black person to have decent housing, health care, etc., he or she must perform way above normal standards (standards not set for white people). Blacks, non-Black people of color, and whites have all asked me if I am mixed, or even from this country, because I don't act "ghetto."

Reflections on Sunnydale

Four years ago, after my mother died, I returned to Sunnydale, visiting from New York City where I now attend grad school. I am amazed at how trapped I still feel anytime I spend time there. The projects are more than a physical location, they're also a state of mind, and the experience stays with you long after you leave them. Even now, whenever I hear a loud noise, I startle, thinking it's a gunshot. I went back with my friend Jennifer and visited the family that now lives where my mother and I used to live: a grandmother, mother, and daughter. The mother actually remembered my mother and me from when I was little. I was surprised at how different their place looks from when we used to live there. She told me I could visit anytime. After chatting with them, I left, knowing I would not be back.

On my visit I recognized a woman I had gone to middle school with, repeating the pattern of many women there—

welfare, living in the projects. I spoke with her, but we didn't have much to say. I learned that a childhood friend of mine had been murdered in a shootout. During that visit I felt that Sunnydale could be anywhere in the United States, in any Third World country; it will never be seen on any postcard from San Francisco, and remains unseen by the elite within the city. I left Sunnydale that day feeling grateful that I was able to escape from the prison I called home for twenty-three years.

A CATHOLIC LEG

TERRY RYAN

MANY CHILDREN GET THE SHOCK OF THEIR LIVES WHEN THEY DISCOVER THE truth about Santa Claus and the Easter Bunny. My greatest shock, which had nothing to do with fiction, came when I realized that our family was poor.

The news should have come as no surprise, considering that my parents, Evelyn and Leo (Kelly) Ryan, had ten children to support on Dad's meager pay as a machinist in the small Midwestern town of Defiance, Ohio. Still, the precise scene that triggered this awakening is lost to me; in retrospect, many would serve as appropriate epiphanies.

Was it the day in early August 1948 that Mom's labor pains began, and she and Dad raced in our old jalopy not to the hospital, but to the bank to borrow twenty-five dollars?

Twenty-five dollars would pay at least part of the hospital expenses when my mother finally gave birth to her seventh child, Michael, later that day. My parents knew from experience that the total bill would be sixty-five dollars—it had been sixty-five dollars in 1944 when Bruce was born, and in 1946 when I was born; it would be sixty-five dollars in 1950 when Barb was born, and in 1952 when Betsy was born. In 1937, 1939, 1940, and 1942, when Lea Anne, Dick, Bub, and Rog, respectively, came into the world, the bill never topped twenty-three dollars and fifty cents. Only in 1954, when the last of the ten Ryan babies, Dave, was born, would the price shoot up to a phenomenal ninety-five dollars.

Was it the moment in the early fifties when I noticed I happened to be wearing everyone else's clothes, and always had been?

My wardrobe consisted of shoes my older sister Lea Anne had outgrown, shirts and pants formerly worn by my four older brothers, jackets and winter coats donated from relatives as distant as an aunt's sister-in-law's adopted daughter.

Or could it have been any Thursday afternoon in the mid-fifties when I witnessed my lilac-perfumed and white-gloved Aunt Lucy pull up to the curb in her forest green DeSoto to take my mother grocery shopping at the A&P?

It took all those years of Thursdays for me to understand that Aunt Lucy didn't just drive my mother downtown to the market. She in fact paid for two shopping carts of food every week, without fail. My mother was shy in the face of such generosity and chose from the shelves only the most vital and inexpensive items: flour, soap, sugar, bread. It was Aunt Lucy who went hog-wild, filling the carts with hamburger, chicken, eggs, tomatoes, fruit, cereal, cookies, ice cream, sausage, and soup. By the age of ten, I realized that without the weekly visits of our beloved aunt, we would surely have gone hungry.

Then again, how about the night when I was closing in on seven years old and stood in the doorway of the kitchen watching my burly red-headed father drink himself into a raging stupor, as he did every evening, on whiskey and beer?

In his twenties, Dad played the violin and sang with a roving dance band. I don't think he ever imagined he'd eventually have to forfeit his free-as-a-bird life of laughter, drink, and dance to toil in a machine shop forty hours a week.

It occurred to me then that he was consuming something far more dear than alcohol. At least a third of his weekly paycheck evaporated in this way, and perhaps more. Not to mention the effect of the drinking on his disposition. He roared his way through the night, a shot glass in one hand and a beer bottle in the other, in a mad monologue that could be heard a half a block away. An inebriated Dad was, as my mother used to say, "about as affable as a bee-stung bear," a generous quote that makes him sound almost charming. He certainly could be—when he was sober, when he put his mind to it.

He had an Irish love of words and music, and a talent for entertaining that had surfaced when he was quite young. In his twenties, Dad played the violin and sang with a roving dance band that toured northwestern Ohio. I don't think he ever imagined he'd eventually have to forfeit his free-as-a-bird life of laughter, drink, and dance to toil in a machine shop forty hours a week.

Granted, my father worked hard every day, under pre-OSHA conditions—no ear plugs, no goggles, no heavy aprons, no steel-toed shoes. As a machinist at a locally owned plant called Serrick's, he tended a stationary screw machine ten times his size that consumed buckets of oil and melted solid bars of metal, re-forming them into bits of useful hardware, such as screws, nuts, and bolts. Serrick's had a score of these metallic monsters, lined up in rows, forming a perfectly aligned orchard of steel. Their collective vibratory roar was known to loosen leaves from neighboring trees.

Dad would arrive home every afternoon with hot-oil burns and bits of metal embedded in his clothes, skin, and hair. The grease, which caused boils on his wide, pink, freckled arms, never washed out of his work shirts and pants. His shoes fairly squished when he walked. He once dropped an unwieldy hunk of heavy metal on his feet, crushing his shoes and maiming his toenails for life. But he never missed a day of work because of drinking.

One of the most memorable benefits of Dad's job, at least as far as the Ryan kids were concerned, was the annual Serrick's summer picnic. While the adults hung around in the shade of tall, sprawling oaks drinking beer and eating ham sandwiches, the kids clawed their way through twenty square feet of ankle-deep sawdust that had been salted with nickels. Six-foot-long coolers held free icy-cold bottles of pop in every flavor. Each of us drank as many as possible, because opportunities like this were rare. I always started out with Dodger Wild Cherry, moved on to Dodger Cream Soda, and finished up with a large Coke. By the end of the day, my right arm would be nicely chilled from dipping into the cooler so often.

Of course, no matter how much money Dad earned or wasted, having ten kids was almost guaranteed to keep his family living at the poverty level. In a single year, ten trips to the dentist, ten new pairs of shoes, and ten piles of school books would put the jackhammer to anyone's bottom line.

Knowing we were poor, however, didn't make my brothers and sisters and me any less happy. In the days before public assistance, Defiance, Ohio, was a good place to grow up in if money was short. The local Lions Club bought our eyeglasses—no small expense for the five of us who needed them. St. Mary's Catholic School waived the annual fees so the Ryans could attend parochial school. Friends and relatives (like Aunt Lucy) were always there to help out.

But the real reason we were a positive-thinking group was our mother, Evelyn Ryan, a woman of high energy and great mirth. Her main creative outlet, aside from having produced the ten of us, was her talent for winning contests. What she called her "knack for words" brought cash and furnishings into the house. In the contest boom years of the forties, fifties, and sixties, magazines and supermarket aisles were filled with product entry blanks, offering big prizes for clever jingles and twenty-five-word-or-less statements on why Dial Soap or Kellogg's Corn Flakes or Heinz Ketchup was the best of its breed. My mother's attention to detail—like noticing that Tootsie Rolls were divided into one-inch segments—was one of the keys to her success. This entry was worth ten dollars:

For chewy, toothsome, wholesome goodness
Tootsie Rolls are right—
Lots of nibbling for a nickel
And they show me where to bite.

How she found even the time to think clearly in a house with twelve people, most of them under the age of ten, I'll never know. Mom scribbled funny verse and contest entries while ironing, while cooking, while sitting in the back of the church at Sunday Mass. What she didn't find humorous in the world, including her own financial need, could fit into a teacup.

Going, Going, Gone!
We can't take it with us—
That much we all know;
My trouble's been keeping
The stuff 'til I go.

Mom won cars, trips to Europe and New York, TVs, radios, clocks, watches, cameras, bicycles, thousands of dollars in cash, and every appliance we ever owned—from toasters to coffeemakers to blenders to refrigerators. Thanks to our constant financial difficulties, she had to sell the largest prizes to keep the family afloat. Smaller cash prizes were used to pay off medical bills and to spring kids' raincoats and shoes, boys' shirts, and girls' dresses from the limbo of layaway at the local JCPenney store. Beyond the dollar value of all the wins, they instilled in my family a belief in miracles, which buoyed us in hard times.

My mother, five years younger than Dad, was born in 1913, the year Congress imposed federal income taxes. The year Henry Ford pushed the "on" button on the first moving assembly line, and the year a Model T automobile cost four hundred and forty dollars. This was also the year that workers' wages averaged just under three dollars a day, a loaf of bread cost a nickel, a dozen eggs cost a quarter, and a quart of milk cost a dime. A dollar could feed a person for almost a week.

Mom's contest wins brought in a lot of needed money and prizes, but neither her wins nor Dad's weekly paycheck could keep up with leapfrogging expenses. By 1944, after seven years of working at Serrick's machine shop, Dad's take-home pay was $3207.46, just over sixty-one dollars per week. With five children and a wife to support, he must have found it daunting to make ends meet.

In 1954, he would be trying to raise ten children on almost the same pay. Forget making ends meet. Those ends were moving in opposite directions.

Still, the truth is that Kelly Ryan did not enjoy labor—whether he was paid for it or not. He worked at Serrick's from eight to four because he had to. Anything beyond that—

mowing the lawn, mending a cracked stair step, fixing a broken lamp—was, to Dad, a useless and falsely pious enterprise.

He liked to take the family for car rides in the countryside when the weather was balmy and the crops were high. We headed out one warm Sunday afternoon, piling into our old blue-and-white Chevy Bel Air, leaving behind appliances in various states of disrepair and a fragile screen door hanging from its frame by a thread. Two blocks from home, Dad spied a middle-aged man raking up leaves from an otherwise pristine lawn and said, in all sincerity, "That sonofabitch thinks he's gonna live forever." He could not fathom personal industry.

Dad also believed that if he had to work for a living, then no other living being should be exempt from the same nine-to-five fate. He envied and despised our cat—a petite black-and-white alley vagrant—and shut her out of the house because, as he often reminded us, "She's too goddamn lazy. All she does is lie around all day." He really meant this. It did no good for one of us to point out that her job was to lie around all day. "The hell with her! Let her work for a living, like I have to, and see how she likes it."

The first house I have any memory of inhabiting was a small, two-bedroom rental on Latty Street, an old and quiet avenue lined with majestic maple trees. The rent came to sixteen dollars a month. My brothers and sisters and I slept in the single upstairs bedroom spread among two double beds and several cots. The house had no bathtub or shower, so those who were young enough to fit took baths in the kitchen sink. My mother washed clothes by hand in an old wringer washer and then dried them on a clothesline suspended between poles leaning at a precarious angle in the back yard. Her work, physical and mental, never stopped.

Who'd trade
Peace of mind
(To most rich men
Denied)
For all of their
Worrisome money?
I'd.

She knew her life would be a lot easier with an automatic washer and dryer, so she won a set in a 1953 contest. Along with those, she won five thousand dollars in cash, using most of it as a down payment on a four-bedroom house a few blocks away. Four bedrooms and a bathtub! We finally had a home that could accommodate all of us. There was still no privacy (with three kids per bedroom, none of us even had a dresser drawer to call our own), but no one cared.

When, twelve years later, my father secretly took out a four-thousand-dollar second mortgage on the house and couldn't pay the money back to the bank, my mother won another huge contest in the nick of time to save the house from foreclosure.

Thus, over the three decades from 1940 to 1970, our family hopscotched its way between destitution and deliverance. Some days, we didn't have enough money to pay the milkman; other days, we could have sent him to Europe, all expenses paid.

My parents were apparently destined for financial insecurity—even with no children left at home to support—all the way to the end of their lives. In 1973, at the age of sixty-two, Dad retired after thirty-three years of working at Serrick's. He had been diagnosed with diabetes a few years earlier, but the condition remained manageable as long as he spent a third of the day working and a third of the day sleeping.

Once retired, though, Dad devoted even more hours of the day to drinking, and his circulation slowed to a crawl, causing festering sores on his feet and calves. By this time, Mom worked as a clerk at the JCPenney store and raced back and forth between the Men's Shirts and Pants Department and home, where she tried to heal the leg ulcers with an infusion of aloe vera gel and golden seal.

But in 1974, despite Mom's efforts, one of Dad's legs became gangrenous and had to be amputated. The night after the surgery, the phone rang, and Aunt Lucy, who had kept Mom company at the hospital and driven her home, picked up the receiver. One of the local priests, calling from the hospital, asked to speak to Mom.

"Mrs. Ryan," he said, "we need to know where to bury the leg."

"The leg," Mom repeated. She had no idea what he meant.

"Yes," he said. "Your husband's amputated leg. We need to know what you want done."

"Well, don't you just . . . uh . . . discard it?"

The priest fell silent. Mom, fearing she had said the wrong thing, added, "I mean in some final . . . respectful manner."

"Oh, Mrs. Ryan," he said. "No. It's a Catholic leg and has to be buried in consecrated ground. You understand."

But Mom, who was raised Methodist and converted to Catholicism only when she married Dad, didn't understand. "Consecrated ground?" she said. "You mean like a cemetery plot?"

"Well, not a whole plot, necessarily, but in a portion of a plot in the Catholic section of the cemetery."

Mom could see the dollar signs adding up. "Egad, Father, you mean a full burial? With a casket? With a headstone?"

"No, no, no, Mrs. Ryan," he said. "That's not necessary. Don't you already have a plot at Riverside?"

"Well . . . no," Mom said. An expense like that was the least of her worries. "I guess Kelly and I have been too busy paying off the debts we've accumulated while alive. I'm sorry, Father, you've got me flustered. I'm afraid I'll have to think about this and call you back."

Then Lucy, who had overheard Mom's half of the conversation and immediately guessed Father's half, laughed and said, "Oh heck, Evelyn, just toss it in my plot."

And so they did. With requisite ceremony and little expense, a small but deep hole was dug in a corner of Lucy Agnes Moore's personal plot in Riverside Cemetery in Defiance, Ohio, and the remains were interred.

Aunt Lucy died in 1989 and was buried in the same plot as her brother's leg. Dad died in 1983, and was buried in a plot the Ryans were eventually able to afford. Mom died in 1998. Evelyn and Kelly Ryan rest side by side in the cemetery, about ten yards west of Dad's Catholic leg.

DEEP CLEAVAGE, BLACK DRESSES, AND WHITE MEN

VIRGIE TOVAR

CLASS IS MAINTAINED THROUGH A SERIES OF SUBTLE AND DENIABLE ACTS.

Wearing a white T-shirt that was chosen to indicate tasteful restraint, but with a signature stitch or subtle insignia that communicates that this is no regular T-shirt. No, this is a $300 T-shirt. My friend Sophie calls this look "aggressively casual."

The way that one responds to the question "How are you?" is a sure sign. It's like a tiny test at the beginning of each interaction, gauging who it is you're dealing with: They say "well" if they are a refined cosmopolitan and "good" if they're not.

Smoking is a telltale sign. A white man who smokes nervously and is very handsome is probably class jumping.

The pathological inability to be rushed no matter the circumstance is a dead giveaway. A woman who can't be convinced to please quickly finish the last sip of her cocktail is a woman who grew up with at least one generation of wealth ahead of her.

A woman who can't be convinced to please quickly finish the last sip of her cocktail is a woman who grew up with at least one generation of wealth ahead of her.

When someone says she went to college "back East," this is pretense, a fauxstab at middle-class humility by not naming the Ivy League college she attended. It's a coded phrase meant to indicate an assuredness that is so unshakeable that name-dropping isn't even required.

Tasteful hints of cleavage that court an air of mystery are an absolute must (upper class). Never more than half an inch, which indicates an undisciplined relationship to desire (working class).

If you want to pass as upper class, never, under any circumstance, be fat.

And always wear black. Especially at parties. That is what respectable women do. This was a lesson I learned not too long ago. I want to tell you that story.

I'M A 250-POUND BROWN WOMAN WHO GREW UP IN A MEXICAN immigrant household in the suburbs of the Bay Area. I was raised by my light-skinned debutante grandmother from Monterrey, one of the northernmost cities in Mexico (her proximity to the U.S. border revealed itself in her European features and reputed snobbery) and my dark-skinned grandfather, who pulled himself out of poverty and into gold teeth, a mortgage, and a champagne-colored 1993 Ford Thunderbird.

I was raised by my grandparents, but I am technically a third-generation American. I am the generation that was supposed to be seamlessly absorbed into U.S. culture. My grandparents didn't have money; assimilation was my inheritance.

My homelife was emotionally volatile, with decades of unresolved trauma trickling down. Alcoholism, colonialism, war. Is rage epigenetic? Is sadness?

I wanted to love my grandparents, but that felt dangerous, like I was walking along the lip of an emotional black hole with incredible magnetism. So I became consumed with the escape that academic ambition promised. I went from a mostly immigrant, brown, working-class suburb in San Pablo to rich, white Berkeley (I didn't know the people around me were rich; I didn't know how to read the signs back then). Eventually I moved to San Francisco, got a decent job, and started writing.

I THINK THAT MY ATTRACTION TO WHITE MEN BEGAN HAPPENING around the time I moved to San Francisco. My pussy became my conduit of class mobility. Class is racialized and so of course my desire became inscribed with a racism that is very old. I didn't know it then, but my sexual desire became part of a global history of that same war that had ravaged my family—the war for the domination of people of color by white people, of women by men, of land by all of us; we all become soldiers through our frenzied drive to survive. How does a clitoris know how to maintain colonialism? It's magic.

And this brings us to the black dress.

I had just started dating a lawyer.

"A white lawyer!" my friend squealed as we walked arm-in-arm down Valencia Street. "Girl, have his babies immediately."

My friend is a black punk who escaped the stultifying homophobia of the American south. He also seemed to understand my pussy's potential for creating a legacy that would take me farther from my family, farther from him. The pain of this class migration is never discussed. Upward mobility takes us away from the place that we came from and the people who inhabit that place. It's understood as positive by all parties involved because, theoretically, we can all "come up" together. In my experience, however, much is lost along the way.

My boyfriend had invited me to his firm's Christmas party, and I didn't know what to wear. I sensed that there was some unspoken set of rules regarding clothing at such an event, but I had never been closer to the epicenter of white respectability.

I reached out to my friend, a white feminist with a PhD, who is married to one of those tech money guys.

"Oh, we wear black," she replied. "Our job is to fade into the background." We. Our.

I was surprised by her response, and thought maybe she was following the rules too closely. I don't know. I mean, a bright red mod dress with a poinsettia lace shell felt more than appropriate to me. I mean, it was festive and had a boat neck. Like, the kind of neckline that people with boats have. I began internally bargaining.

Meanwhile, I made an appointment at a nail salon, a gossipy place close to my house. These nail technicians had been hired by the boss lady, who was filled with Botox and venom. The kind of woman who would cut you with a tiny razor she held between her teeth at all times if no one were watching. The kind of woman who's had to do things, too, to be here.

"What's wrong with him?" the woman who was filing my nails asked after I told her why I was getting my nails done. I imagine this question may have been prompted by my being unshowered—I'd been short on time and hadn't bathed before my appointment—and fat. He must be some kind of murdering domestic-abusing mutant, because normal lawyers don't date fat brown women who don't shower before their nail appointments, right?

Since I was getting judged anyway, I figured I would vent about my outfit conundrum. So I told her about the office party.

The petite white woman with curly hair sitting next to me asked demurely, "What firm?"

I told her where he worked.

"Oh my god. My boyfriend works there, too!" she sang. "Definitely do *not* wear red. I am wearing a simple knee-length black dress." She finished by pointing to her ears: "We get to have fun with our earrings" and then wiggling her fingers "and our nails." We. Our.

I DIDN'T WEAR A BLACK DRESS AFTER ALL, BUT I DIDN'T WEAR the red dress either. I wore an off-white silk blouse and a burgundy leather skirt. I got my hair blown out into a circa-1960s style, a nod to the dress that got left at home.

When we arrived at the party on the top floor of the San Francisco Ferry Building, I took the room in quickly and immediately understood what was happening.

The dresses were like a silent demarcation—a color line. The (few) women who were lawyers and the women who were partnered with lawyers were slender, had little or no makeup on, and wore black. The secretaries and female staff were black and brown, mostly plus size, and wearing leopard print minidresses, vinyl pumps, dangly earrings, stiletto nails. They looked more like me. They were certainly wearing what I would have preferred to wear.

I'm not sure if what I saw was some perverse drama that I had transmogrified within my mind, or if it all really was so obvious, so absurd, so awful, so contrived, but I was ashamed for knowing. I was sad that I would never unknow.

The theme of the party was "Caribbean Vacation," an inside joke enjoyed by men who take great pride in working too much. I can imagine them chuckling: "This taco is the closest thing I'm going to get to a vacation as long as I'm taking all those depos!" Somehow "Caribbean" translated into steak fajitas and other anglicized Mexican food. I was into the spread but I was unsure if they knew this was not the right food or if they thought the whole equatorial world was a homogeneous territory, and that anything made with a tortilla elicited the sense that one was on a holiday.

The white women in black nursed a single, tiny flauta and anemically sipped on a glass of wine.

The darker, fatter women in bright dresses laughed with their mouths open, requested cocktails at the open bar, and enjoyed the food.

Just like always, I felt caught between these two kinds of women and the worlds they represented. One that meant nothing but that I'd been taught was everything. And one that I didn't know how to want because it was too terrifying. It represented self-acceptance, the end of striving, the power of knowing that I had already won the race that never seemed to end, a return to the kind of femininity and love that reminded me of home, which had hurt me so much.

I wanted to want to pass, to belong. I mean, this was adulthood, right? I'd always known that someday I would have to put away the "childish trappings" of loud music, shared apartments, huge rings, huger sunglasses, getting high on the beach, talking about my bowel movements at dinner parties, having my tits out, tiny shorts, cracking up when something was funny, calling it like it is, never getting confused about what was a hustle (this was a hustle). I'd imagined that someday I would shed all those desires and wake up one morning with the genuine thought, "Ya know, today I'd like to wear a necklace with a delicate rose gold chain that features a ¼-inch earth-toned stone." Or, "Oh my, aren't Eileen Fisher scarves just wonderful?"

But I also wanted to dance. The firm had hired a DJ for the party, but only the staff—none of the lawyers or their black-dress-wearing attendants—danced. I kept looking over at the women on the dance floor, smiling like they were the ones who needed assurance, trying to give them some kind of signal that I was like them. I wanted to tell them how good they looked. I wanted to tell them how bomb their shoes and earrings and nails were. I wanted to tell them how they should get down on the boss's dime because fuck these people.

I tried to get Boyfriend to dance. "Come oooonnnnn," I whined, like this was my last chance at redemption. I dragged him onto the dance floor. He stood there bouncing awkwardly—painfully aware that he was violating the class laws—while I got down. The only one from the black-dress crowd on the dance floor—imposter revealed.

No, they knew before then.

I TRIED TO CONVINCE MYSELF I WANTED TO STAY IN THAT WORLD. Boyfriend bought a home overlooking the Pacific and gave me a key. We had a housewarming party. I made jokes about becoming a Xanax-and-chardonnay addict.

I told my friends it would be so fun. They could have all the shit he'd bought for me. Wouldn't it be great? I was happy for them. But my friends genuinely heard the story I was telling. My friends are feminists, queers, weirdos, sex workers, activists. The kind of people who don't wear black. The kind of people who are magic. They told me I deserved better than a big house with lots of things. They told me "There's no language, no framework, for choosing this when you have access to that. You have to write it yourself." They told me I was valuable on my own, and they didn't need things as much as they needed me to be O.K. They told me they would be there when I was ready to leave.

I started telling my grandma I wasn't happy, that I couldn't stay with him. She started giving him our family heirlooms. Her allegiance to my financial security was stronger than her wish for my wholeness.

The day I finally left, my friend Sara had come to see me. We met in college, where she used to do Jim Carey impressions. She sat with me at the kitchen table, where you could watch whales with a small pair of binoculars that Boyfriend had been given at his housewarming party.

"I feel like it's wrong to leave like this." I had packed all my stuff in my car, my grandpa's car that I inherited after he died. The champagne-colored 1993 Ford Thunderbird.

"It seems like maybe you've been wanting to leave for a long time," she says.

But I also wanted to make it work. I wanted to bury myself and live in a big house with a white lawyer and have his half-white babies and disappear. I'd teach those babies how to sing Raffi songs. They wouldn't know Spanish because I don't know Spanish. They wouldn't like big earrings because they never would have met their grandfather. I would trade my hooptie in for a Subaru. I would make sandwiches. My cleavage would disappear. So would my cheetah print wedges. My Mexican-ness would be nothing more than a passing point in conversation.

Instead, I got in the car, turned it on, pulled out of his driveway for the last time, and drove down the coast. Down my favorite curve in Highway 1, where the Pacific Ocean suddenly appears and becomes all you can see for miles and miles.

MY FATHER'S HANDS

DAISY HERNÁNDEZ

MY FATHER IS IN HIS SIXTIES. HE IS A TALL, THIN MAN WITH AN ALMOST bald head. He has a small beer belly beneath his white cotton T-shirt. His hands are never empty. There is always a cigar, cigarette, or beer can in them. He's handsome, and he's an alcoholic.

Years before the Cuban revolution, my father, then a teenager, saw a soldier in the hills where he and his family picked coffee beans, cut sugar cane, and raised pigs. He liked the soldier's matching jacket and pants, the uniform's sense of purpose. My father didn't want to be a farmer. He wanted something more. He wanted to be on the side that won.

Some years later, he got the uniform and fought against Fidel Castro. Unfortunately, he only talks about it now when he's drunk, slurring the words and his history into a number of possibilities. But this much is true, he says: It isn't easy to switch sides in a war. So he left the island along with the United States embassy workers and came to New Jersey, where he cut hair, opened a bakery, painted houses, closed the bakery, and cut wood. By the early 1970s, he had settled into factory work and married my Colombian mother.

He returned to visit Cuba once before NAFTA and told his cousins how good work was in the north. His job was to stay up through the night with a textile machine. He'd replace needles that broke and alert the bosses to any problems. It was he and the night and the deafening sound of the machines. He didn't need more than a few English phrases. On weekends he made extra money helping with plumbing, electricity—those many jobs where a man is always useful.

Then, in the nineties, factories began closing. My father's work hours were cut from twelve a day to eight, and then six. I began finding him home at all hours of the day and night and after a while I stopped asking why, because all he would say was, "*Se terminó el trabajo* (the work ended)." The work ended like a novel, its mournful last page close at hand.

When he wasn't on the clock, my father drank. His hands would point at me and remind me to study hard because "you don't want to end up at a factory like your mother and me." Even before I understood words and phrases like "manual labor," "working class," and "alcoholism," I knew how they felt: like my father's hands.

Parts of my father's hands are dead. The skin has protected itself by hardening, turning his large hands into a terrain of calluses and scars, the deep lines scattered on his palms like dirt roads that never intersect. His hands are about power and survival, my first lessons about class. The dreaded question comes on Wednesday afternoons when my father drags the trash cans to the curb. That's when the Colombian lady across the street pushes her screen door open. She's noticed my father at home lately and asks him about his job. When he tells her the factory is closed *por ahora*, she tilts her head like she already knew. "*Y estás colectando?*"

What she really wants to know is if he's collecting unemployment benefits.

"There's no work to be found," my father answers. His pants are falling from his narrow hips and he yanks them up with his left hand.

"*Pero, estás colectando?*"

My father shrugs his shoulders. "*Es la mísma basura.*" It's the same garbage.

He wishes the Colombian lady well. From my bedroom window, I watch him walk into the two-family house he and my mother bought with years of savings. In the basement, he finishes a six-pack of Coors beer and listens to Radio WADO. He's found a store down Bergenline Avenue where the price of beer drops when unemployment rises.

AT CATHOLIC MASS ON SUNDAY, THE COLLECTION BASKET MAKES the rounds. The Cold War is over, but the world is still divided into good and evil, democracy and communism, Catholics and others, the ones who give and the ones who collect. It is a simple arrangement. One ill-spoken word could damn you to hell, communism, and poverty.

There is some comfort in knowing even God has to collect. But still the church's collection basket makes me anxious. I'm afraid we don't have money to give because, when it comes to Strawberry Shortcake stickers, my mother says we don't have the money. In church, my eyes rarely turn to her. Instead, I listen carefully to hear whether her pocketbook will join the others to interrupt the church's silence. It does.

The collection baskets crawl down each pew and swallow the sounds of crinkled dollars and jingling coins. I hold two, sometimes four quarters, excited to throw them into the basket. The tap dancing of those coins into the basket makes me feel we are as good as any of the families here with five-dollar bills in their hands.

Spanish is a Romance language except when you're trying to make ends meet. The Spanish we speak is a language in which life is reduced to talking about what you need, what's working and what isn't. *No hay trabajo. Media libra de chuletas. Basta ya. Van pal'iglesia. Estás colectando?*

Are you collecting? The rest of that sentence, the words "unemployment benefits," never makes it into Spanish.

Are you collecting? The rest of that sentence, the words "unemployment benefits," never makes it into Spanish. There is no need for it, because everyone here knows what is meant when the question is asked. No one says we're "receiving" or "getting," because no one here really believes we have a right to that money. You're "collecting" because you don't have work. You're one step away from *la gente en* welfare and two steps away from the old lady at Port Authority who's collecting pennies from commuters. Even in English, we call it "unemployment benefits," thinking it's a benefit to get something back from the work we do.

I live with Spanish, with coming home to find my mother watching a telenovela. Her factory shut down for a few days and her Spanish words are to the point. "Your father's in the basement. They called from work, said to not come today."

In the basement, my father talks to Elegua, an Afro-Cuban god without hands who lives in a clay dish and opens doors. He has only a face, sculpted into a round pointy crown. When my father is collecting unemployment, he feeds Elegua more candy and espresso so the god will open the door to another job.

Elegua is better than learning English. He's the god of trickery and journeys; you can trust him more than English words that change tenses, don't sound the way they look, and get turned on you at the factory.

As a child, I am drawn to Elegua and his candy dish. The Cuban women explain to my Colombian mother that Elegua loves children and that's why I'm spending time with him. But they are wrong. I am a practical child. Elegua's the god who opens doors and I am desperately trying to get away from my father's angry, drunk hands, and the feeling that our destinies are scribbled in the square opaque windows of my father's factory. Because Elegua is the god of crossroads, I imagine he understands the contradiction of my growing up: that I want to escape from my father and also take him with me, that I want to flee my life without leaving Papi behind.

I am meant to escape. Everyone tells me so at the barbecue for my mother's birthday. "Girl, you're going to be something some day. You're going to make it. Irma, will you look at this thing the *nena* wrote for the school paper, her name and everything. Girl, you're going places." No one ever says where I am going, but they are sure that a place is waiting for me.

By the time I am nine and translating my report card for my father, I know he is not going with me.

IN ELEMENTARY SCHOOL, I HEAR THAT AMERICANS ARE TRYING TO keep up with a family named Joneses. The Joneses are a mystery of the English language. My mother says she's never heard of "*la família Yoneses*" and I should quit worrying about what everybody else is doing.

In our part of the world, no one is keeping up. We belong to a community based on the fact that we are all doing bad. When someone does a little better, there is an unspoken betrayal. You smile at them and when they leave, you talk about how they are lying to get welfare checks, working *por la izquierda*, putting on airs. When you are the one doing better, you sit at your kitchen table and say, "It's incredible but true. Any little good thing you got, somebody else wants." You talk about how *celoso*, jealous, people can be. It is easier to say that people are jealous than admit they have a right to want something better.

It takes years for me to understand that the Joneses happen only in English, in houses where people cook in one room and eat in another. The Joneses don't happen where people are called "white trash" and "spics," "welfare queens" and "illegals." And no one ever asks the Joneses if they are collecting.

When someone asks my father how he is doing, he looks at his hands, studies the scattering of black scars and the dryness of the skin. His answer is always the same, "*Ahí, caballero, en la mísma lucha.*"

When I ask him what it means to say you are in the same *lucha*, my father says it means you are doing the same old thing. Years later in community activism, that's all I hear, that we're in this *lucha* together. *Lucha* means struggle, someone tells me. The same old thing, *la lucha*. I sit at a lesbian collective meeting, my hand clasping my pen tightly. It's hard to explain how in one moment, someone can translate a word and your understanding of your family and your history can be turned around.

In the mid-nineties, the *lucha* changed. Neighbors began talking about working as home attendants. The closed factories began outnumbering the ones that stayed open, and the new jobs were in cleaning floors and baby diapers and serving food. Men from Central America arrived, renting the first floor of our home, eight men, two bedrooms. The whites who could moved out. People came from all parts: Mexico, Pakistan, Brazil, India. The men waited at the street corner for construction work that barreled down the street in blue pickup trucks. In our basement, the Spanish newspaper was marked in red ink with circles and X's.

My father survived the onset of NAFTA because of the Cuban revolution. A political refugee, he was entitled to citizenship and the unemployment benefits that carried us between his jobs. The newer immigrants and those who came from other countries didn't have his privileges.

At the unemployment agency, he sat alongside African Americans, Pakistanis, Dominicans, and Nigerians, and they learned the English words for the work they did, and how to spell them. "Embroidery." "Seamstress." "Machine operator."

Factories closed for a week, a month, forever, and we waited for the phone to ring. The calls came randomly. At first the voices were Pure American English, a language that rarely falters. It begins with a "hey, your dad home?" and ends with a "thanks."

I was never to say that my father was out looking for another job or that he'd found one, part-time. I was never to reveal anything over the phone. Just take the message.

Sometimes the factory had not closed but "tell your dad to come at eight, not five, tonight." Or, "Tell him we need him tonight." "Tell him to call us next week." "Tell him he can file for unemployment."

As the years passed, the factories changed hands and the callers changed. The American voices disappeared and were replaced by an English that stumbled all over itself. "Halo, Ignacio?" No, he's not home. "Eh, tell him, no work, eh, come ehere efriday."

Even the unemployment agency changed to a new dial-in system to collect unemployment benefits. The brochure came in Spanish and English.

My mother studied it carefully. My father made the money and my mother handled it. She wrote the checks, paid the bills, and completed the forms for unemployment with me. My father's hands could do many things, but handling money was not one of them. Making phone calls was not one of them, either. His hands would wake me up with a gentle shake. He'd still be sober. "Your mother called unemployment and couldn't get through. Come on, get up, call them."

The dial-in system was fabulously efficient. Much more so than the factories that closed.

If your social security number ends on an odd number, call on Tuesday. If it ends on an even number, call on Thursday. Enter the weeks for which you're claiming.

The dial-in system was clever. They said it was to help us, to avoid waiting at the agency for a long time. I suspect it was the best way to handle a possible riot as the economy switched from the manufacturing to the service sector. Not making a trip to the agency meant you wouldn't have to see in one room how many other people were going through the same thing. When you did show up (because the phone system didn't work), there were fewer people, even though back on your street you knew it was more people than that. You began to doubt yourself. Maybe it wasn't so bad.

Not going to the agency meant you could avoid seeing the pain of other people. You didn't need to know English to understand the agency man telling someone on the line that "no, sir, according to this you have nothing left to collect." You didn't need a translation for the immigrant man's English words, "But I no find job." And then came that dreaded English word—"welfare." "Sir, I'm gonna need for you to get off this line because we can't help you here. Get on the line at window four and you can talk to someone there about welfare."

Calling in, you could avoid that man's eyes, the way his brown body, sheltered under five layers of clothes against the winter storm, turned away and left. You could avoid looking at his empty hands. You could avoid thinking about what would happen one day when none of us could collect.

The only thing I feared more than my father not being able to collect was time spent collecting. At least when there was work he wasn't around drinking and yelling at me as much. The world was cruel to him, yes, but it was hard for me to be angry and afraid of an abstract idea like "world." It was easier to be afraid of my father's hands. Easier to be angry when the blistered and swaying drunk hands slapped me on the back of my head. And there were other emotions that came more easily than anger: fear and guilt. Fear that life would always be like this—at the mercy of a factory closing, a paycheck arriving. Guilt because I—with my English words and schooling—would one day lead a different life than his. I just had to get there.

For about a year, I worked at McDonald's. I worked the register and got free meals. My job meant that if I set my mind to it and flirted with the right managers, I could become a manager too, with paid vacation, paid sick time, and a steady paycheck. So I watched my classmates play softball, run for student council, and drive their new Nissans. I'd get home and change from my Catholic uniform to my McD's one. If I worked enough hours, I made as much as my mother did at the factory.

On Saturdays, the manager created competitions to make us work faster. "The register that makes the most money before noon gets two tickets to Loews movie theater!" It was the first time anyone had ever referred to me as a machine. But I just smiled politely. I was proud of learning the register, its grid of prices. Big Macs, Large Fries, Apple Pies. But the manager was right. In a matter of months, I had become a machine. You had to shut down some part of yourself to the sexist jokes, to your hours cut when a new manager took over the schedules and didn't like you. The job was like walking on a tightrope without a net. You are up in the air alone. Interacting with other people is an act of acrobatics. You never know who will start talking shit about you. You never know what will piss off your boss. You never know why they sent you home but not the others. A wrong word could mean your hours the next week were reduced from forty to thirty-two.

It's hard to write this part of the story. It's the part of the story I never talk about with my New York friends, writer friends, community activist friends, with anyone. We act the same—like we never worked with our hands. Sometimes we mention in conversation that we worked menial jobs, we stripped, we waited tables, we worked fast-food jobs, we cleaned diapers. We use those middle-class words to describe experiences that are not middle-class. But we don't know how else to talk about them.

It's hard to write about how quickly I moved that Saturday, how jealous and ashamed I was when I came in a close second for those tickets. It's hard to write about burning my fingers at the fry machine, how the grease of the place sticks to your skin, how you take the money you earn to the nail salon and get long acrylic tips and for a moment forget you are at a job that slowly turns your hands to cardboard. And it's harder still to know that a good number of people don't work and live like this. Harder still to know those people are your teachers, your friends who live in towns where McDonald's aren't even allowed to open.

In college and after, there are other jobs, the ones you really talk about over dinner with friends. The job at the library, the newspaper, the publishing house. But after years of numbing myself to working-class life, an alcoholic father, a fast-food job, it isn't easy to make myself feel something. I am too used to a world where trips to museums are something you do on class trips in high school. Our passions weren't work, but what we saw on the Spanish news, our romantic lives, losing weight, getting pregnant, waiting to love, wanting to be loved, the specials on Bergenline, the freebies at the Macy's Clinique counter with a purchase of $19.95. We talked about dreams, where we'd go if we had all the money in the world, who we would marry if we could pick anyone.

Those office jobs after college meant walking into a place where people didn't dream like that. They had jobs they liked, money-market accounts, paid vacation time. Dreams were something that actually happened. No one talked about buying a Lotto ticket.

More than anything now I am trying to feel something rather than numbing myself to the gap between my father and me, between the past and the present. I get a paycheck for writing newspaper articles about unemployment, while he works part-time as a janitor. Friends tell me to feel accomplished, that my résumé is a reflection of him, his sacrifices and triumphs. That's probably true, but it doesn't resonate.

The only things that do make me feel something are art, writing about him, loving him, taking pictures of his hands, listening to him tell me I should photograph this one scar on his index finger. He can't remember how he got it.

WHAT'S THE QUESTION AGAIN?

AYA DE LEON

MY MOM WAS AN EXOTIC DANCER. A PHOTO OF HER HUNG ON THE WALL OF our living room, a black-and-white photograph from her early twenties, sitting in profile with bare feet tucked under her. In the picture, she's wearing thick black eyeliner and a sandy brown pixie haircut. A light-skinned Latina, her face looks like Jane Fonda circa 1960, but her leopard-print bikini looks more like Wilma Flintstone. The most noticeable feature in the photo, however, is the boa constrictor snake wrapped around her arm and neck.

My mom grew up in the projects in L.A. Her European-American father was an alcoholic, and her mother was a Puerto Rican immigrant with a thick accent who couldn't get work other than cleaning houses, even though she had a college degree. My mother grew up smart but poor. When she left home she worked many shitty jobs, including as a telephone operator for "working girls" and a retail clerk at Frederick's of Hollywood. Being an exotic dancer wasn't by any means the worst job she ever had. She'd tell me stories, laughing about how the snake helped keep creepy guys from messing with her.

I would often wonder if I could make more money with my body. I always knew I could, and that I would, if I needed to.

My mother walked around naked in our house when I was a kid, whether she was thinner or thicker. She never seemed self-conscious about her body, and I grew up feeling the same way. So when I was in college and tired of working for minimum wage, I would often wonder if I could make more money with my body. If I took my clothes off for pay. I didn't do it. But I always knew I could, and that I would, if I needed to.

I WENT TO A PRIVATE UNIVERSITY WHERE MY FINANCIAL AID covered room and board as well as books, so I was never hungry or in danger of homelessness. But there wasn't a lot. I was raised by my single mom, and around junior high, my father stopped paying his court-mandated child support.

My dad visited me at school during my freshman year of college. I was not yet eighteen and he was still responsible for me. We sat at an outdoor cafe where I ordered a croissant, then anxiously peeled off the layers and put the little half-moons of pastry into my mouth while my dad drank coffee. Between sips, he told me that he was going to start paying me the child support directly instead of to my mom. Then he gave me $300, his monthly payment, in cash.

I had never had that much money in my hands at one time. We left the cafe, and he went with me to open a checking account. When I deposited the bills, I felt like a millionaire. I thought, *maybe I can focus on school*, and *maybe I won't need to get a second job*.

The next month, I waited for another check. It didn't come, and it didn't come the month after, or the month after that. The balance dwindled. Finally, I closed the account. I felt so humiliated. How had I let myself be such a sucker? I knew my dad didn't keep his promises. Why did I let myself believe this would be different?

When I graduated, I asked him not to come to the ceremony. "Graduating college is the hardest thing I've ever done," I told him. "I want to celebrate with the people who helped me do it."

I REMEMBER AROUND THAT TIME, A BUNCH OF FRIENDS WERE sitting around and one of them asked us all the following question: "If there was no danger involved, would you have sex with an average-looking stranger for $10,000?" I didn't understand the question. Of course I would. I was already having sex with average-looking near-strangers for nothing.

And the sex itself was by no means its own reward. I was looking for that attention I couldn't get from my dad. Of course the sex didn't satisfy me, because I wanted a deeper connection, even as I was scared to be vulnerable. But I was captivated by the intensity of the attention I got from men by dangling the prospect of sex. *I know you want me* felt infinitely more safe and powerful than *I need you to care about me*. So I developed a sexy girl persona who had a bunch of casual sex and didn't get much out of it.

For $10,000? What's the question again?

I HAD WORKED A NUMBER OF DIFFERENT JOBS THROUGHOUT college, many of them work/study jobs that were part of the financial aid package. One year, some friends and I stayed on campus during spring break and cleaned bathrooms in the dorms for extra cash. It paid much better than the work/study jobs, which were never hard, but they were mindless, isolating, and boring. I'd sit at a desk in a windowless basement and check out films to students in the semidarkness.

It was in that basement where I decided there must be something more interesting and lucrative I could do, and I seriously considered the idea of taking my clothes off for pay. I proceeded to call all the art schools in the area to ask if they needed models. Sure enough, Boston University needed models for art classes. Easy money! And I didn't even have to pose nude—it turned out that you could be paid the same amount for modeling with your clothes on, so I did that. Only once, though. I found the inability to move to be somewhat torturous. How ironic that stillness, not nudity, was intolerable.

MY FIRST JOB OUT OF COLLEGE WAS AS A COCKTAIL WAITRESS. I learned to multiply by $2.75 because that's what most of the cheap beers cost at the club where I worked. That place paid subminimum wage plus tips. I never bothered to pick up my last check because they calculated our taxes based on wages plus estimated tips, and then took the full tax amount out of our paychecks. The checks were for around $2, as much as the subway fare would cost me to go to the restaurant and pick it up.

Raised by a mother who had grown up poor, I'd been schooled in the mythology that getting a degree would open doors for me, and on the other side of those doors was the good life. I didn't realize that it was also necessary to have access to people with resources and influence who could help you move your life forward. I didn't realize that college wasn't only about studying; it was also about networking. But as a Black/Latina woman, I found college hostile. I focused on surviving and getting out. It wasn't until afterward that I really gave a thought to what was next, and by then it seemed like it was too late. So there I was, waiting tables with my Ivy League honors degree.

Like so many folks raised working class, I've had to figure out how to navigate my way through the world of work without much mentorship. My life has generally felt economically precarious, in part because I chose to be an artist, but also in part because I carry inherited anxiety about survival from my mom. Only now, decades after I graduated college, do I have a life that is beginning to look somewhat middle class. I'm married, have a kid, and my partner and I both have steady, white-collar jobs. I even drive a boring, reliable family car.

Recently, I've landed my dream career, writing novels. Really, it's a dream side-hustle, because I can't afford to quit my day job. In my novels, I have found myself often writing about women who do sex work. At first, I had no idea I was writing about my family. It wasn't until years later that I realized my writing about sex work was part of my family inheritance. Curvaceous young black and Latina bodies learn quickly that the society is ready to monetize our tits and asses. Working-class females learn that our bodies and our sexual labor are considered our biggest financial assets.

So I have reclaimed the sex work lineage in my family, and I write about a sex worker crew. My books have become an intentional version of the young woman I used to be, who deploys her sexy girl persona for the greater good. These steamy novels are a stealth social justice organizing strategy for my community. The book reels the reader in with a promise of sexy, uncomplicated pleasure, but the politics of the book hit hard: feminist health care, wealth redistribution, and labor organizing. So, in spite of my class upward mobility, I maintain a connection to the sex work community, and I stay committed to hustling justice for my poor and working-class folks.

WINTER COAT

TERRI GRIFFITH

"DO YOU GET ENOUGH TO EAT AT HOME?" THE SCHOOL NURSE ASKS, AS SHE sets the clipboard in her lap and looks at me earnestly.

"Yeah," I answer, not really sure what she's getting at.

"Did your mom make you dinner last night?"

"Yeah."

"What did she make?"

"Macaroni and cheese."

"Did you have breakfast this morning?"

"Uh-huh."

"Do you have breakfast every morning?"

I don't know why the nurse is asking me these questions. I don't know why she came to my classroom and in front of my classmates asked Mr. Logan to have me excused. But it's obvious from the sound of her voice and her overly controlled tone that she thinks my mom has done something wrong. Maybe it's me who's done something wrong. Her questions make no sense. How can I give her the right answer if I can't understand why she's asking me these things? I don't want to get my mom in trouble. She wants to know what my mom feeds me. Maybe my mom cooks the wrong food. Maybe I eat the wrong things. Maybe it's because I didn't finish my vegetables last night.

"Well, I'm concerned because you're underweight. You're very small for your age."

The nurse was right about that. When I was in elementary school, I was small for my age, but it wasn't because I didn't eat. I ate fine, in a '70s sort of way. Beanie Weenie. Meatloaf with corn. Frozen fried chicken with salad. I never once went hungry. But there were a lot of times when I complained and didn't finish my dinner, especially after the third night of split-pea soup with ham hocks and carrots. Now, when I look back on the times when I think I might have gone hungry, my mom and I conveniently went to dinner at her best friend's house. For a while, we ate dinner at her house a lot.

Just four years later, in the sixth grade, I would be the second-tallest girl in the class, complete with boobs and a period. I was never the skinniest girl in my grade; Sarah was. Her parents were rich. I bet no one pulled Sarah from class to ask her what she had for dinner last night.

When I started kindergarten, not one of my classmates had parents who were divorced; I was the only one. But by the time I was in junior high, more than half the class came from single-parent homes. Without exception, all of us kids were raised by our mothers, who worked two, sometimes three jobs to support their families. It was just my mom and me, and although things seemed bad, other families had it much worse than we did.

The 1980s were hard on the Pacific Northwest economy. Many people lost their jobs, the timber industry collapsed, lumber mills closed, the salmon runs were depleted. The families in my neighborhood were all tied to these economies—families I considered rich because the kids played on soccer teams, bought their school clothes at department stores, and lived in houses their parents owned. Now I understand that these families weren't rich at all. Their fathers were longshoremen, their mothers worked at the paper mill, their family owned a fishing boat. All of these people had working-class jobs, hard jobs that extract the life from a person. I guess I was lucky when I was young—my mom had a white-collar job working for the Department of Corrections. Even though it sounds fancy, it didn't pay much—but she made ends meet. Then my mom got laid off, and life for us got much harder.

The thing about being poor is that you know what it means to be poor—and there's always someone poorer than you. For all my funky hand-me-down clothes from my mom's best friend's children, there was always some girl in class with greasy hair who smelled like pee and didn't have a winter coat.

My school didn't make it any easier to be poor, though at first glance it might have seemed as if it did. We "free lunch" kids stood in a separate line and had to give our names to the Lunch Lady, who checked us off her list. For what? To make sure we didn't get two lunches? The Lunch Lady said we had to stand in this "special" line so that she could keep track of which kids "took advantage" of their free lunch. It always felt as if we stood in that line to make sure there was no confusion between whose parents could pay for a hot lunch and whose couldn't.

The really poor kids got free breakfast, too. This was the worst of all possible elementary school fates—being tagged "free breakfast." When my mom told me that I was to leave the house a half hour early so that I could have breakfast in the cafeteria, I nearly died. I didn't want to go, didn't want to face the other kids I would be joining. Their parents didn't have jobs, they came from huge families, and at least a fourth of them were from the giant government-run Children's Center, two blocks away.

These Children's Center kids had, as the principal described in a special assembly (without them), "behavioral problems," and weren't able to stay in regular foster homes with real families like other boys and girls. Back then I didn't know who those kids were. I do now. Who's labeled "incorrigible" at six? What kind of fourth-grader is unplaceable in foster care? Kids who are abused sexually and physically, kids who are drug-addicted at birth, that's who.

I was terrified of what these children might do to me. They were animals—we had been warned. Would they beat me up? Stab me in the leg with a fork? I would be one of these "free-breakfast" kids, and now everyone would know it.

At first, I simply didn't go to school early. I took my time, played in the gully, sat in the alley outside my best friend's house until she left out the back door so we could walk to school together. I waited out the breakfast portion of my day, but I was a little girl and I got hungry. Free, hot breakfast was waiting for me if I were willing to claim it.

The free breakfast my school provided was too tempting to resist. Pancakes, syrup, bacon. Scrambled eggs, sausage, cinnamon rolls. My mother's idea of a yummy breakfast consisted of bland puffed rice, dreary puffed corn, and the narcotic winter favorite, Cream of Wheat with a square of melty margarine on top. Of course, I gave in. Even so, I still had my pride. I wasn't about to give up my breakfast secret that easily. My technique was this—I shoveled the hot breakfast into my mouth as fast as possible, then shot my hand into the air and waited as the lunchroom attendant came and checked my plate to make sure I'd eaten every bite. If I ate fast enough, I could make it out of the cafeteria and into the hallway before the regular kids started arriving. That way, everyone would think I was just an early riser and not the "free breakfast" I really was.

"COPS ARE GONE," RICKY YELLS FROM THE TOP OF THE STAIRS.

Who knows how long we have been in that basement room, all thirty of us, crowded together, waiting in the dark, the only sound that of someone taking a slurp from their beer can. It happens all the time. The band is playing upstairs, someone spots a cop car, and we all rush to the basement before they make it to the front door. The band members always stay upstairs and pretend it is an innocent band practice that is making all the noise.

"No, officer, there isn't anyone else here. Just us." Then Ricky mumbles some promises of a quieter rehearsal, and the cops leave.

I head back upstairs to look for Kelly, a girl I can't quite call my girlfriend because we are both closeted and we only ever kiss when we both get drunk enough to make out in a back room or some car, anyplace our boyfriends won't catch us.

The two of us talk about music, smoke cigarettes, discuss what edgy book we've just read, drink even more beer, and make plans to see whatever cool band is playing in Seattle next weekend. What we never talk about is our future, what college we will go to, what we want to do for a living, what we want to be when we grow up. From where we stand, it is impossible to see our way out. We keep our talk simple. Even if we do harbor secret hopes for what our lives might someday be, we don't share them. I know it is foolish to think I can climb my way out of this ditch and into the American Dream. Eventually, Kelly will stumble back behind her drum kit and the band will start playing again (a little softer this time), until the early hours of the morning.

It's hard to plan for the future when there isn't one. If you didn't have money and never expected to, you joined a band, went to shows on the weekend, drank cheap beer, and listened to hardcore.

It's hard to plan for the future when there isn't one. What did the world have to offer us working-class kids? In the eighties, if you had money, or thought you might ever have money, you were preppy: applied to business school, liked Michael J. Fox, read books by Bret Easton Ellis. If you didn't have money and never expected to, you joined a band, went to shows on the weekend, drank cheap beer, and listened to hardcore.

With few exceptions, none of us were bad kids. Well . . . sometimes we behaved badly, but there was never malicious intent. My friends moved into "the city" (population 75,000), where I lived. They came from rural areas, towns with 5,000 people, the neighboring islands, and the reservation. A bunch of scruffy punk rockers who worked as cooks, like me, or at the lumberyard or shake mill. For some of my friends, life didn't turn out too well. Many of us ended up strung out, in prison, or dead. Some got permanent work at the paper mill or airplane factory. Others became teachers, professional musicians, and parents.

What's a young dyke with no role models to do? How could I conceptualize a future that I had never seen? I had met a couple of grown-up lesbians before. There was Butch, who worked at our neighborhood gas station. I never thought much about it, just figured she was another girl with a boy's name, like Sam or Pat or Stevie. It wasn't until high school that I realized "Butch" was probably not the name her mother gave her. Then there were the ladies who worked at the paper mill. Flannel shirts and shift work, that's what I thought being a lesbian meant. I couldn't be a lesbian; I wasn't anything like those women.

My mom raised me to be middle management, to go to college—community college first, then state college (scholarship willing). I was specifically brought up to not go to work at our town's ubiquitous factories. Pink collar over blue collar any day! I was also raised to not take risks, not because my mother thought I was incapable of taking care of myself, but because she believed that a steady paycheck was the key to a happy life, which it just might be. My mom wanted my future to contain all the things she didn't have. New clothes, the ability to pay the electric bill when it was due, the luxury of hoping to someday own my own home.

Without the protection economic stability provides, there is no room for failure. I had no room to fail. My mother had no room to fail. When a child is raised to always take the safe road, the intention is to make that child's life easier, to empower her with financial security. But really, it only teaches her that she can't do anything.

I STOOD ON THE TRAIN THIS MORNING WEARING MY NEW WINter coat. I live in Chicago now, and it's the coldest place I have ever been, below-zero cold, cold that can kill you. The kind of coat you wear tells everyone on the train who you are. She's poor: She's wearing two lightweight coats that look like they came from a thrift store, or "resale shop," as they're called here. He's rich: His coat is black leather and lined with fur. She's working class: Her coat is warm and puffy, but a few years old and machine washable. In Chicago your coat is a statement of your material worth. You don't really think the stars of hip-hop videos wear those down-filled or shearling coats because they're cold, do you? Before I moved to Chicago, coats didn't mean anything to me.

Chicago has poor like I didn't even know existed—public housing projects that go on, literally, for miles; families of six living in one-bedroom apartments and people sleeping under the elevated train tracks. And there's rich like I've never seen, except on television—women and men wearing full-length furs on the street, three-hundred-dollar dinners for two, and eight-million-dollar condominiums. Oprah lives here!

My new coat cost two hundred dollars. I've never spent that much money on an article of clothing in my life—not shoes, not even a bridesmaid's dress. My coat is black wool, with shiny buttons. It's fitted, long, and has an opulent black fox collar and cuffs. I wear this coat to job interviews, out to dinner, and sometimes to parties. I will not wear this coat to bars or shows, anywhere I think will be too smoky or where someone might slop beer on it or burn me with a cigarette. This coat will be expensive to clean.

Despite its warmth and evident beauty, my coat makes me uncomfortable. I have never owned a coat so nice and I am afraid the other passengers know this too. I look around the train to see if anyone is looking at me. In this coat, I feel like a spectacle.

What do people think of me? Do they think I'm rich? Am I rich? I bought this coat, even though it was with a credit card. I'm scared to wear it too much because I don't want to wreck it, or wear it out, or spill something on it. My girlfriend says, "Wear the coat! It's not made of gold," though to me it is. Can the people on the train tell that I am ill at ease in something so costly? Do they think I am trying to pass for something I am not? Am I trying to pass? I worry most about what the working-class people on the train think. I want to go up to everyone wearing a faded old coat and say, "My clothes, what I have on underneath, all of it comes from the Salvation Army! Really, this is a fluke. Really, I am one of you." I don't say these things, but I think them.

Is this what growing up "without" means—that I can (almost) afford a fancy coat, but can't enjoy it? What about the American Dream, the theory that with hard work and perseverance people can transcend the class into which they are born? I want to believe in it, but I don't. Class is about more than money; it's about safety and security, knowing that what you have today, you will have tomorrow. It's about having faith and feeling safe in the knowledge that when my coat gets worn out, there will be other coats.

When I get home from work, I place my new coat on a wooden hanger, and hang it on the shower-curtain rod. I do up all the buttons, smooth it out, then go over it with a lint brush. I am going to make this coat last forever.

THE JUST-ADD-WATER KENNEDYS AND BARBECUE BREAD VIOLENCE

POLYESTRA

FEWER THAN ONE PERCENT OF AMERICANS BREAK OUT OF THE CLASS THEY are born into. Despite these grim odds, people like my parents still base their entire lives on the dream of class jumping. The television gospel told them it was not only possible, but normal. To not increase your wealth was more shameful, to my family, than a brown lawn, unusual offspring, and unemployment combined. They considered every day that went by without a yacht and a swimming pool embarrassing. And everyone else in the neighborhood who didn't miraculously obtain a new Cadillac or a vacation home at the beach, or who was still working construction or driving a cab, was equally shameful. To my parents, every day in this working-class neighborhood was temporary. It was just a matter of working hard enough.

My parents didn't think of "class" as an ingrained culture, as a part of who they were. They had no pride in where they came from, only in where they dreamed of going. They were two out of millions who erased themselves for the homogeneity of TV-inspired blandness, smiling into cereal commercials like adoring fans. The American Dream. Television was a sick ritual for people like my parents. After dinner my father would peel down to his undershirt and light up a cigar, clenching it between his lead-and mercury-filled molars (some strange side effect of serving in the military). He reclined in his personal chair, his oiled black pompadour shining in the TV's light. My mother perched posture-perfectly on the sinking couch. They pored over images of gluttonous mansions and commented on how they would arrange the furniture in such a place, what color scheme they would apply to each room, where to put the remote control, rotating fireplace, and wishing fountain. They wanted every car in every car ad, every diamond ring, dinette set, wide-screen television. Their idea of "rich" wasn't being able to afford furniture from somewhere other than Sears, but being able to afford the most expensive furniture, and a lot of it, from Sears.

My parents had no pride in where they came from, only in where they dreamed of going. They erased themselves for the homogeneity of TV-inspired blandness.

Every weekend we went to my grandparents' house, no skipping allowed. If we were all dying of pneumonia, we were still required to go, or suffer the wrath of Thelma and Johnny. My father's parents were hard-core about their son becoming a millionaire. They had been through the Depression. Their lives reeked of financial failure and poverty—one big drag for all the world to know about—and now it was up to my father to save them from dying in shame. These were bitter people: The old man chain-smoked and drank canned beer while the woman actually wept over "the mixing of the races." They had been robbed and screwed over, or had screwed themselves over, so many times they had developed a fear of hordes of non-Caucasians entering their row house at night to kill them and make off with their nicotine-stained divan, their silver utensils (which were hidden in the wall of the cellar), their rechargeable electric grass clippers, their monogrammed pen and notepad set from 1939. Even in the worst dry spell of generic-cigarette half-price sales, their son would surely save them. Even if they ran out of green olives for their "special occasion" martinis, even if the TV went on the fritz during *The Lawrence Welk Show*, my father would save them. Even if my grandfather slipped away into an alternate plane, humming songs of Austria while belching up bile and swallowing it again, which he did, my father would take care of them. And so he did.

My parents had two kids, both of whose purpose in life was to become rich. The torch had been passed. It was now my parents' goal to mold us into something "rich," to strategically insert us into the upper crust, thus ensuring a wealthy retirement. Their first attempt at this was to enroll my sister and me in private school (from which we were rapidly ejected, since they couldn't pay for it). They insisted this would give my sister and me a much better chance of marrying some sweaty-palmed old-money boy when the time came. Unfortunately, they overlooked the fact that these rich children wanted nothing to do with us. The rich, like those mysterious Masons and the CIA, have seriously tight-ass circles that not just anyone can penetrate. This really messed with my sister's mind; she was in a constant state of agony. All the other girls in her classes had designer jeans, and my sister was the only one in the whole school suffering without. My mother sewed fake patches onto generic jeans, but this only made the whole thing worse when a classmate ratted her out.

Next they enrolled my sister and me in ballroom-dancing classes at the country club, where we were nearly guaranteed to become "cultured" and "civilized." This move was in part a response to my natural attraction to vandalism and dirt-bike ganging, which severely infringed upon my parents' princess dreams. At the country club, they thought, we would learn how to charm the hell out of the rich, play their games, rub elbows with the next generation of money people. Membership was by invitation only. We were the only kids in the classes whose parents weren't members. These kids came from well-known, old-money families. For them, the waltz and the fox trot were some sort of perverse "fun," where they got dressed up and twirled around a ballroom like royalty. To me, it was horror.

Everything about me showed I didn't belong, from my inappropriate, not-quite-formal tube dresses to my macramé jewelry. (Our clothing arrived in the mail from our Canadian cousins—hand-me-downs from the hinterland—and was better suited to square dancing and getting beat up in a big city.) My mother tried to compensate by hand-sewing me the gaudiest satin and lace dresses. She went for the latest fad: low-waisted, poofed-out dresses that made me look like my torso was twice as long as my legs, like some shapeless, disproportionate mutant. She even bought me little white gloves—like the JonBenet freakazoids wear on the creepy children's talent shows in Atlantic City—and patent-leather Mary Janes.

Once a week, my mother, in her beige polyester London Fog–style overcoat and metallic-blue eye shadow, her helmet perm and beige secretary pumps, drove me up the winding road of manicured grounds in our clunking Toronado station wagon. At the top of the hill sat the Colonial castle within which waited the liverwurst-scented old ladies with castanets and the teeming brood of the stinking rich of Delaware, all prissied up like miniature millionaires. There I slouched in a "period" chair against the wall while all the little boys in suits and gloves chose all the little girls in velvet and lace, leaving me to sit there for the entire time. One of the deeply creased, too-much-sun-in-a-lifetime old ladies sometimes forced one of the boys to dance with me—more as a punishment to some lazy boy than to help me. Their parents were Du Ponts and oil tycoons, and one boy, his rubbery hand like a hoof on my hip, said to me, "You'll never marry one of us."

"I know," I said, and I wasn't offended. I had gone to private school with this arrogant little boy, who was commonly known as "Booger" for his ever-sunken finger in his ape-shaped right nostril. I just wanted to go ride my bike down a steep, rocky embankment, give someone a black eye. Instead I found myself seated at a very long table, my eyes full of what seemed like hundreds of sparkling utensils. We were "quizzed" during each course of a sickeningly massive meal as to which utensil to use. My hand trembled over the fourth fork from the left, the knife located beside the smallest plate, expecting a slap on the wrist from one of the wrinkled mummies. Each item presented by some annoyed waiter was smothered in hollandaise. Boiled meat and hollandaise. String beans and hollandaise. All this in preparation for a final banquet and ball, to which the parents were invited to get loaded and watch their kids do the bunny hop. I was thankful to find out we weren't invited, but my sister wept bitter tears for days. Her sorrow worsened when we found out we were the only ones enrolled in the classes who weren't invited. My parents complained that they hadn't gotten their money's worth for the classes. They couldn't understand what had gone wrong.

MY MOTHER WORKED AT A BANK WITH BRUCE WILLIS'S MOM. Every day, sucking up minimum wage, my mom told Bruce Willis's mom about how she would be rich someday. My father worked at Sears with Elvis Presley's drummer. He did the same. He asked a customer, "You want us to rotate the tires while we're at it?" and then told Elvis Presley's drummer how he would be rich someday. Elvis Presley's drummer rotated the tires, smiled slowly at my dad, and went to the bar after work like everyone else. The reality of working shit jobs somehow didn't sway them from their delusion. Instead of resenting the rich, who would never let them into their club, they talked about them as if they were family: "George Wellingham III got a new Porsche!" "Ivana Porkroll is divorcing Richard—it will split the families for sure." "Little Rutherford Hoggerton has been chosen to go to the military academy—did you hear, girls? He's your age!"

Every day when I walked to school I walked past the private school, where my friends and I were harassed by a bunch of horse-faced blondes in team shorts, holding on to lacrosse sticks. It just so happened that the school had constructed a pedestrian tunnel under the road, and a few kids from our school had been killed crossing the street there, so we opted to walk through the tunnel. "No white trash allowed!" they would bellow, threatening to call the cops. The property between the private school and the public school was all Du Pont estates. One day an old lady in the back of a limo pulled up next to us on the street and told us she didn't want us walking past her driveway—on the public street. She wrote down our names and said she would notify the authorities of our intentions to rob the Du Ponts. My associates and I decorated the walls of the tunnel with slogans, such as, Rich Fucks, Fucking Snobs, Eat Shit Moneybags.

My father quit Sears and plunged headlong into sales. Real estate. He worked seven-day weeks for the same or less pay than the Sears job. It seemed like a turn for the worse, but then, rather suddenly, my father started making money. A lot of money. They went on vacations to the Caribbean (a perk from the company for high sales), from which they returned with rolls of photos of dangerously sunburned, severely inebriated Realtors and their spouses, their heads wrapped in wet towels, their swollen faces sucking on mixed drinks; dance floors full of drunken, Delawarean Realtors screaming into the dirt under a limbo bar; Realtor wives shielding their eyes from the camera while Realtor husbands bend them over folding chairs for a mimicked spanking.

My parents gave in to the reality of their long-awaited fantasy. They bought stuff like crazy. They bought rental properties and a beach house, new cars, an antique car. They hired a maid. They bought my sister and me jewelry and clothing, furniture and toys, new everything they could get their hands on. The hand-me-down hoe-down clothes were quickly replaced by rich-kid fashion, which sent me into a junior-high identity crisis. For the first time I realized I was trapped between classes—considered too uppity by the poorer kids, and having nothing in common, except the same uniform, with the richer kids. I sat alone in my suddenly made-over bedroom, stripped of its chaotic wall of Scratch-n-Sniff stickers, Scott Baio and *Dukes of Hazzard* posters, and giant carnival-prize stuffed animals. My completely whitewashed new room, with custom-designed cabinets, framed fine art posters, and a vanity full of gold jewelry and make-up, was completely foreign and frightening.

I hid the jewelry, afraid it would be stolen and my parents would never forgive me.

Now we were going to brunch at ritzy hotels, driving to Pennsylvania to try the latest new fancy restaurant. It was all an abrupt turn from my mother's infamous boiled-chicken dinner. It seemed like one night we were carefully removing the nearly liquid white skin from a boiled chicken leg, swallowing half a softer-than-butter boiled onion—and the next night our dinner was being served on fire. My father, who was almost always embarrassingly drunk and loud at such occasions, was glaringly out of place in his red suit and American flag/bald eagle tie, using a long umbrella with the head of a duck as a cane, his lips pulled back in a huge, unconvincing smile, framing half an unlit cigar in his teeth. Yet there I sat, in some hideous pastel dress and flats, watching the waiter's mouth as he asked us to quiet down/put out that cigar/pay the tab and leave.

At home in our big house flanked by new cars and gaudy decoration, our better-than-thou-neighbors' posturing was scandalously tarnished by barbecue bread violence. My father insisted on a loaf of bread being present at meals, to save him from choking (some weird thing from my grandmother). During the summer we usually ate outside on our deck, which was highly visible to the entire neighborhood. By the end of the meal, my drunk-ass dad would almost always be ready for a fight—any fight—and he usually let loose on the bag of bread first. Neighbors would stare shamelessly as my father pitched the loaf into the chain-link fence, where it would explode into a tragedy of misshapen slices while he bellowed, "I bring home the bread!" This popular exclamation was heard by all on many occasions from my father: from the second-floor balcony in his underwear, from the lawn with shotguns in each hand, from his car wrestling with my mother for the keys.

THEIR DREAM FOR US HADN'T DIED. HIGHER EDUCATION, TO MY parents, was still a way for their children to jump class. And so, when the time came, they insisted we go to college, though both of us protested. We would be the first in both of their families to go. They were sure that with our first step on campus we would meet scads of tall, block-jawed future doctors and lawyers who would fall in love with our cultured, high-class charm as soon as they laid eyes on us. My sister's Mohawk and chain-smoking of menthol 100s, and my common pastime of watching TV flat on my back with a bowl of cereal propped between my breasts, somehow didn't dissolve their mirage. These were just phases that would end with high school, they assured us. Apparently they looked at me and saw a potential cheerleading sorority girl in the raw, ready to be polished for action at any moment, unleashing those two years of private school and dance-class etiquette.

No matter how hard they tried to turn us into just-add-water Kennedys, all of this posturing failed, and so did college. The bottom line was that we were lower class, and there was no way we could be any different. As we were dragged nearly screaming off to college, the late-eighties economy steadily sank into the toilet. Their rental properties remained vacant, the beach house unrented; the cars wouldn't sell, and the real-estate market floundered. Their debt grew so out of control they were faced with declaring bankruptcy. All of the Realtors from the tropical vacation photos were declaring bankruptcy like dominoes, but my father couldn't deal with the shame. His suicide note was addressed mostly to his parents, and said how he had failed them by not being rich. He also declared his right, in the freest nation in the world, to choose death.

Our family was left in a sinkhole of debt. People came to the house during the funeral to claim cars and to try and buy the house. Everything was liquidated, and we all went our separate ways.

Despite my parents' arduous attempts at my reconstruction, I have retained bits of my native culture that will now be offered up to my daughter whether she likes it or not. Like eating green olives and watching *Lawrence Welk*, dirt-bike ganging and the art of survival in a classist nation, flamboyant American-flag apparel preferably worn in conjunction with a Mohawk or similar angst hairdo, and, most important, keeping a bag of bread on the table—not for fear of choking, or as a festering analogy to money, but to eat.

CAREER COUNSELING

ARIEL GORE

I DON'T LIKE THOSE PEOPLE WHO TELL KIDS THAT ADOLESCENCE IS THE BEST years of our lives.

That's the kind of lie that can really kill you. It's the kind of lie that makes you feel alone in your depression. It's the kind of lie that can scare you for a long time.

There were other lies like that.

"I think I want to be a writer," I told the career counselor at the California junior college where I almost signed up for classes.

I was back living with my mother and stepfather in the stucco house I'd run away from more than three years earlier, trying to pretend I didn't notice the sour stench of my own humiliation.

My mother made fresh zucchini and peach baby food. She painted my childhood bedroom pink. She held Maia in her manicured hands, said we could stay as long as we needed.

But at night she said the opposite. "Everyone," she whispered, "is very embarrassed for you, Ariel."

Who was everyone?

I imagined a whole audience of everyone I'd ever met, spotlight on me, and they all cringed knowing I'd done something terribly wrong.

I share my childhood bed
with the baby
nurse her as we both fall asleep
her body is soft like clay
all hunger

I needed money so I could leave but didn't know how to get any, not with a baby. The jobs I was qualified for wouldn't pay for childcare.

One day I got a chain letter in the mail.

I sent ten dollars to the name at the top of the list.

I added my name to the bottom of the list and sent it off to ten unsuspecting members of my stepfather's church congregation.

Surely, if I waited, I would receive $10,000 in ten dollar increments—small white envelopes in the mail. I awaited my $10,000, but all that came in the mail was a Stonehenge postcard from the baby's father.

> Dear Ariel,
> In Londontown hanging with Joe Strummer. Almost have the money together for the airfare to San Francisco. Sorry about everything. Let's start new.
> Love,
> Lance

I threw the postcard away.

I'd always had a soft spot for the baby's father. He sang that David Bowie song, "Kooks," in the morning in his sweet London accent, but he was a mean drunk at night, and even though I didn't know about alcoholism yet, I could see that the drinking was getting worse. I could see something else, too—something I couldn't quite put my finger on—something about the way the world kept telling him to "be a man" that frustrated him to the point of violence.

I SAT ACROSS FROM THE COLLEGE COUNSELOR IN HER LITTLE GRAY office. She wore a well-ironed gray suit.

A poster behind her pictured the Everest summit: *Aim High*.

"*Aim high*," I mouthed to myself. I didn't tell the counselor I'd crossed the Himalayas by myself on foot when I was seventeen. Before the baby.

"You know, write?" I said. "Creative writing?"

The career counselor shook her head and her exhale held a silent, bitter laugh. She let the corners of her mouth turn up as she said, "Good luck."

I sat there, not saying anything. I glanced over at Maia asleep in her soft blue onesie in her blue polka-dot stroller. She didn't mind sleeping in that stroller, didn't even mind sleeping cradled next to me on park benches on warm summer nights, but I knew she'd grow and need more.

The counselor leaned back in her gray chair and adjusted her gray jacket and tilted her gray head to the side like she was maybe trying to pop a vertebra in her neck.

"Miss Gore." She looked down at the piece of paper on her desk, like maybe she was trying to remember my first name. "Ariel."

She said, "Miss Gore, you have a child to take care of now. You really ought to make an attempt to come down to earth and think about that. You need to think about your child and you need to ask yourself how you're going to make a living."

She pointed to a small stack of brochures on that gray desk: *Become a Certified Electrician.*

Her words made my heart contract, but I still felt compelled to politeness.

"Thank you," I said before I grabbed the handles of the polka-dot stroller. I opened the door to get out of that airless office, held it open with my hip as I maneuvered the stroller.

The career counselor didn't rise to help me.

"Thank you," I said again, and I let the door slam shut behind me.

Why did you say thank you, *Ariel?*

You're an idiot, Ariel.

Shut up, only crazy people talk to themselves, Ariel.

I pushed the stroller, my pace quickening. My mother's words rattled in my head, too.

I'm nineteen and I've already lost, and there's no unlosing now.

You chose this life, Ariel.

You're on your own, Ariel.

Everyone is very embarrassed for you.

Like I'm nineteen and I've already lost, and there's no un-losing now.

THE CEMENT PATH LED PAST CEMENT PILLARS, PAST SQUARE GARdens, toward a green expanse. "Aim high," I whispered under my breath, then tasted the rage. "That fucking bitch." My walk morphed into a run. Tears streamed down my face. I pushed the stroller. Maia slept. She kept on sleeping.

Maybe the career counselor was right. Maybe I didn't know how to live. I didn't know how to make a living. My parents had always been broke, my mom making art no one wanted to buy and my step dad selling books for minimum wage, but they had a house. I wondered what it would feel like to have a house.

I had to make a living. Becoming an electrician sounded cool, but becoming an electrician scared me. Electrocution scared me. I felt too anxious and afraid—I should have told that counselor—to be trusted with live wires.

I felt like a sucker for telling that counselor woman what I wanted, what I wanted to be.

I felt like a fool for wanting something I had no right to want anymore.

MY DEAD ABUELO NEEDS A SUGAR DADDY

JULIANA DELGADO LOPERA

WE DIDN'T HAVE MONEY TO BURY HIM OR BUY FLOWERS, THAT WAS THE REAL problem. My grandfather, El Paisa, was the first one to die en Estados Unidos, mysteriously and abruptly, and nobody knew exactly what to do.

At the hospital, after staring at the cold, yellowing body, with the protruding nose not covered by the white sheets and becoming the joke that night amidst the endless tears—*how are we gonna find a casket big enough to hold both him and his nose? Maybe we can get some money for that nose in this hospital, maybe a gringo wants it*—after every woman in the family circled him, once, twice, three times, after the pastor elevated one of those prayers on the afterlife, after all the tías yelled at the doctor and female wails reverberated like ping pongs all over Miami, after Mami fainted and Grandma lost control of her feet, there was the inevitable List of Things to Do After Death.

My family is no stranger to this list. Every two years or so, someone inevitably dies and we plunge into this ritual, this process, all over again.

We understood The Economics of Dying in Colombia, but here it was a mystery. We'd been in Miami for three years, Mami didn't have a job, and this was our first American funeral.

Dying is *gratis* but the rest is business.

Dying is *gratis* but the rest is business, *mi reina*. And of course there had to be a funeral, of course it had to be pomposo and grand. *Con flores y, si se puede, mariachis y quien tuviera un dinerillo para pagarle un par de lloronas. Como Dios manda.*

After all, this was El Paisa: Gabriel Lopera Lopera, father of five, grandfather of nine. Motherfucker from day one, now gone. We had to send him to Papi Dios like a prince, *pa' que sí lo reciban. Pa' que Diosito le de gold wings y un puestico especial.*

IT DEPENDS WHO YOU ASK, BUT NOBODY REALLY KNOWS EXACTLY how El Paisa died.

According to Tía #1, he was rushed to the hospital because he was "running out of air." Doctors were supposed to evaluate him and send him home that same day—instead, they sent him to the morgue. When pressed for details, Tía #1 simply shook her head, lit a cigarette, and murmured, I don't know, Juliana. *Yo no sé muy bien.*

If you ask Tía #2 she'd tell you, those *hijueputas* killed him. *Es que tu no sabes la que nos hicieron.* She's visibly exasperated, reliving every second, picking her dry hands. *Se me parte el corazón, se me parte el corazón.*

Tía #3 says they're both wrong. She says he stopped breathing in the middle of the night and nobody came to help him. The nurses ignored his pleas. And the doctors? She chuckles. *Descarados.* They told us it was a heart attack but mi papi had no heart issues, she insists.

Then again, he was old, so who knows.

Then there's the story I heard the day of his death: They transfused the wrong type of blood. El Paisa's blood was O-negative, but the nurses said he was O-positive and filled him up with the wrong blood.

The tías sent people all over Bogotá searching for his medical records so the Lopera Juan Family could sue the hospital, but there was no suing. Nobody could pay for it. We wanted to pay for an autopsy, someone explained later, to make sure they didn't kill him, but did you know an autopsy costs approximately $3,000? We didn't have enough money for that either, so eventually we had to call Tía L.

(Side note: Tía L. A lot of families have one. L is that far away tía who, from the moment she could say *Colombia es una mierda* and *por favor to me don't speak Español*, yearned to be rich and powerful [if possible blonde and white]. Unlike most tías who yearned, slapped-a-bitch, changed their names to attain crumbs of this rich, white life but never got close, Tía L sits at the top of my family's Who's the Bitch with the Cash Flow scale. The epitome of good, successful, white-passing assimilation—without ever dropping that accent, 'cause forgetting your panela roots follows you to the grave. Because of all of this, Tía L walked dignified and earned prestige—adoración, really—in the family and will be called upon throughout the story as the one person who could drop some Gs).

I remember this time in a blur: The perpetual rush of women filling papers, chain smoking, murmuring the loss in shame because there was no money, *mi reina, ni para el casket, ni para* las flowers. We were sending El Paisa to be cremated in the cheapest little hole in the city when he deserved a gold urn and a procession of millions.

I remember Mami, forever pale green and dragging her feet, fainting so often I started carrying alcohol and cotton in my purse. From time to time I slapped her. From time to time I shook her. But Mami could barely take it all.

I can't believe we are not going to properly send my father away, she said.

The impotence undid her.

Let me explain something to you. El Paisa had an insurance plan, not a real one but the underground kind sold by Cubans in certain "clinics" in Miami. The kind that solely exists as a tiny pink card inside immigrant mamas' wallets in South Florida. It exists in every señora's mouth as part of the immigrant advice you receive when landing in The Promised Land. I imagine these underground clinics were created by the Cubans in the early '70s; I can picture the señoras phoning one another, setting up infirmaries so their families wouldn't die just because they couldn't pay the outrageous American health care fees.

My entire family was enrolled in this insurance. Each person paid $20 a month to visit a doctor in a desolate tin house next to the highway with wooden links barely holding it together. It was all super clean but it looked like a Red Cross makeshift tent in some war torn place. Still, I dreaded going to this place. The TV was perpetually on, blasting Univisión or Telemundo so loud I couldn't read, while women yelled at their kids.

It was a reminder of what we'd lost. I had been a privileged teenager once, back home, where we could go to real hospitals. We'd come all the way from Colombia for what? For this? This place held together with babitas? One time, a patient asked the receptionist to put his lunch in the fridge. When she responded that the fridge was full of people's excrements, he said, *no importa, mama*. Put it in there.

My grandpa was insured there, of course. A Colombian doctor worked there sometimes and we all went the days he was available. The problem was that when shit hits the health fan, the $20 pink card is worth exactly that: a $20 pink card. It doesn't cover the ambulance or the emergency room or the tubes to keep you breathing or the exams or the blood transfusion or the aftermath of death. When your homeboy dies and the forms pile up, under insurance you can't just write *I got some pink slip from the Cubans*.

ONCE SHE STOPPED FAINTING, MAMI GATHERED ALL HER STRENGTH and walked to the nearby cemetery with some tías. Someone looked up "cheap funeral services" online, and this somber, gray yard was the closest one to our home.

The smell was horrid, the place buzzing with mosquitos.

A señora greeted us, a Cruella De Vil in black with parted white hair and an air of terrible indifference, and told us the prices.

Like we were picking fruit at the plaza.

Nobody respects your pain in this country. A man is dead and it's like you're at the supermarket or choosing a vacation destination; everyone tries to sell you a different packaged combo. For a burial without the body, you get ten percent off; you can rent the casket for a discounted price, but only for an hour. For $500 extra, you can get two lloronas to honor your dead father.

The entire funeral would cost between $7,000 and $10,000 and we had to pay it up front. *Nada de descuentos, mi reina, que esto es un negocio como cualquier otro.* There are no discounts, because capitalism respects no one and this includes the dead.

At some point, Mami needed to breathe and walked into the cemetery's garden. It was here that Mami talked to Papi Dios; it was here that she reprimanded The Lord for creating outrageous prices when all she wanted was a nice funeral and some flowers. It was here that she yearned for Colombia. *La Tierrita*. The *país de mierda* that held all of our dead in gothic churches and cold cemeteries. All she wanted was to bury her dead with dignity but, in this country, she didn't know how to. In this country dignity has an impossible cash price.

On her way back she stopped by a water fountain.

Dios mio, how is it possible that you will not let me bury my father?

God in His infinite wisdom just shrugged and whispered *it's time to call your Tía L, mami*.

El Paisa wanted to be cremated because it was cheaper. At least, that's what Tía #2 told me. As things go in Miami, one tía knew another señora whose best friend had owned a funeral company in Colombia and was just starting her business in Miami. Tia #2 called her.

Tía #2 is the official family Hustler, known to get people to drop sixty percent of the price plus give her a *ñapa* after speaking to them for fifteen minutes. Homegirl can get you to agree to sell your house in exchange for some eggs if you give her enough time. I've seen her in action. It's mesmerizing. Tía #2 hustled the Colombians, who agreed to drop the price because, *ajá*, we're Colombians, too, and how you not gonna help your own people?

This audacious guilt-trip move (plus Tia L's money) got us three hours in a funeral home where we all cried, wailed, sang, and fainted. El Paisa got three hours in a rented casket, a crown of yellow flowers donated by a cousin, and a last trip to that sad cemetery, where he came out of the crematorium in a brown box.

I don't even know why we paid to cremate him, someone said to me. It's probably only half of him in that box and a bunch of other people.

After his death, Mami kept receiving El Paisa's mail, including endless hospital bills. At some point, she stopped opening them and returned them to the mailman with a note that said *He doesn't live here anymore, he's dead*. Then Mami enrolled all of us into a funeral insurance plan that she still pays for to this day. Because this is not happening to me again, she says.

Now, if one of us dies, you can put us in a casket, add some yellow flowers, light a candle, and call it a day.

REVERSE

SILAS HOWARD

Donut Shoppe, 1978

I watch through the rain-streaked windows of the camper.

The Formica counters in the doughnut shop are chrome-lined, chipped, and faded to the color of Miami pools. Fluorescent lights flicker as the television plays: a blue Cycloptic giant announcing the news of the day: Christopher Reeve plays Superman, Carter meets with Middle East leaders at Camp David, and Jim Jones kills a congressman and then orders his followers to commit suicide. Sun-washed posters along the walls feature colossal close-ups of French crullers, maple doughnuts, and old-fashioneds. A couple sits drinking free refills and contemplating the responsibility of leaving town with a child, a fat golden retriever, seventy-five dollars in their pockets, and the camper. This is their escape hatch—a family vacation, an extended Sunday drive, travel through the nice neighborhoods to envision life in the ornate homes of the well-to-do.

At the doughnut shop that night they decided that, yes, they would go across the country. They would ignore the grinding, almost suffocating lack of money that kept them in a never-ending state of panic, a feeling that staying at home averred. This trip would be a clean slate, a new page, everything still to come. Necessity makes reality real.

I watched the highway from the bed that sat over the cab of the truck. Yellow lines moved hypnotically, miles and minutes passing, boredom into daydream. I wondered, my eyes wide as marigolds, where the dashes of yellow would take us. Like most kids I had ideas of what I wanted to be when I grew up, and many were the usual—veterinarian, farmer, Olympic figure skater. But when things were very chaotic, my ultimate fantasy was to grow up to be a housewife who watched TV, baked, and stayed home a lot. Things must have been bad during this time, 'cause I never remember having the dream so powerfully.

I became allergic to security, as if it might pull me into a slumber and I'd wake up making donuts.

In the end I became allergic to security, as if it might pull me into a slumber and I'd wake up making donuts.

It never occurred to me that taking a family vacation on seventy-five dollars that lasted almost a year was strange until

I talked about it with some friends recently. What, not all families take vacations this way? The "vacation" was scintillating and nerve-wracking. When there was no food, we always had television. Commercials filled with sexy, slow-motion shots of cheesy pasta dishes and tender prime rib steak.

The money lasted from Burlington, Vermont, all the way to that town in Virginia where some pilgrims landed, I forget the name. There we landed, tired, lost, and out of money. My stepmother got work as a cocktail waitress, and my father took a job at the local Red Lobster. The plan? Zoom to California and then drive back home again by the end of that summer. We made it to Atlanta, Georgia, my parents taking work along the way. The trip was extended past Christmas. Our family vacation lasted eight months and caused me to miss most of fifth grade.

By the end of that family vacation, the thing I wanted to be was an actor, California my mythical oasis. It was my obdurate belief that I need only set foot in Los Angeles and all my dreams would materialize. I wanted to be part of the lust-and-danger-drenched Hollywood fantasies that served as our weekend drug. Only I wanted to play the leading man—a role young girls were not encouraged to play.

Hollywood Forever

I now live in Hollywood and, while I'm not an actor, I did act in a movie my friend and I made titled *By Hook or By Crook*, a feature film that ended up winning several awards and being selected for Sundance. When Harry Dodge, my oldest friend and cowriter/director, and I were writing the script, we funded ourselves by hauling garbage. Two small, earnest guys filled with an ambiguous hope, to save people from the clutter of their material goods. There's big money in trash. Our only setback—we couldn't really afford the dump fees. Late at night we circumnavigated the industrial part of town looking for places to "store" our trash. Disposal turned out to be the hardest part of making money. All that effort to save fifty dollars. The risk of police and junkyard dogs. We'd tell people, "I didn't go to college, I went to haulage."

Nowadays I edit the added features that go on DVDs. Mainly I work on horror movies, where the bad girls get killed first and the college students are chased by—as one director put it—"cross-dressing retarded hillbillies." That's me, I think, though most people I know would protest. I need a T-shirt that reads, "No one knows I'm a cross-dressing, retarded hillbilly." The director states that his horror movie is about the generation gap—the youth running from the older, rural folks—but I think it's poverty they're running from. And run they should.

Everything is up for grabs in L.A., even the ground. Los Angeles is a horizontal city on shaky little legs. It is a city with no center, where things are hidden—especially true feelings. A place, they say, where you could die of enthusiasm. I love that about this town. My life as a myth. When trying to have more in your future than you did in your past, a vivid imagination is key. Fake it till you make it. The pathos of endless hope and possibilities, of being taken advantage of, *ahhh*. I could be discovered, maybe, just maybe . . . Yes, I realize "maybe" is a thin thread to hang one's hopes on, but I can still live next to my dreams and visit them—a little like having stuff in public storage.

Every day I wave at the sandwich man on my corner.

I drive by him every day. He stands on the corner with a handmade sign advertising inexpensive lunch specials. I think about his health and the tedium of it all. I think about him when I wonder what my next job will be now that I've moved from San Francisco to L.A. Actually, I don't imagine his face when I think of him, but rather the face of his costume, which is a large (from above his knees to a few feet above his head), sun-bleached sandwich with a shop logo on it. The sandwich is made of bread and floppy lettuce, and on the bread is a big smiling face with two huge eyeholes cut out of it, for the sandwich man to breathe through. His hands are big and padded like Mickey Mouse's, which I guess are the hands that a sandwich would have if a sandwich had hands. I wave to him when I'm stuck at that corner of Highland and Santa Monica.

When the sandwich guy waves back, he seems so enthusiastic that it breaks my heart, although perhaps it's only the big, cartoonish hands that I read as excited. It's quite likely that the guy wishes I'd stop waving at him like some five-year-old at the poor kids' Disney. Probably he should conserve his energy. It can't be good for you, wearing a polyester suit in the middle of Los Angeles in summer, where the temperature frequently rises to 100 degrees. This is a dangerous combination—polyester, holding and shaking a sign, and the desert sun.

I had a friend who worked for an ice-cream shop as a bear one summer, and she had a whole padding of ice that she kept in the freezer to put on for work. "You can faint like *that*," she said, snapping her fingers for emphasis. Another friend of mine appeared on a talk show in an E.T. outfit. He nearly faded away because the costume was basically one of those rubber Halloween masks that almost killed you as a kid, but that went over your whole body. He was hunched over in the thing for an hour, waiting for his turn on the show, and by the time he got up there he was more like a sad, creepy, abused E.T. than the happy, bicycling-over-the-moon one from childhood. He made it offstage before passing out, but ended up, I imagine, depressing most of the audience.

Sometimes I see the sandwich walking home down Santa Monica Boulevard with his big square head slumped down. Of course, the tilt of his head may be a logistical thing—so he can see—but I choose to read it as a guy down on his luck stuck in this dead-end job as a sandwich. I make another vow to bring him a cool beverage with lots of ice. I wonder what his pay might be.

Later

"It's called IWS."

"What?"

"IWS—Inherited Wealth Syndrome."

This young man at a house party is telling me about his job with the Rockefeller family and the counseling service provided for inheritors and their spouses. This service helps with the trauma of having more wealth than you can comprehend; the trauma of feeling unworthy, for instance, since you will never be as great as the first Rockefeller, who made all the money.

"They have parties after these seminars with the staffers."

Oh, the wealthy must envy the staffers—"You make a finite amount of money? That's so amazing. Tell me, how do you spend your paycheck?" my friend jokes.

How many people have this syndrome, I wonder? I guess if you're that rich, it takes only three or four people to make it a bona fide disease. Quality over quantity. It's all about reimbursement, and if it's in the DSM, then insurance has to cover the treatment.

A woman sitting across from me explains her recent money-raising idea. She posted an offer on Craig's List that essentially read, "I will call and insult anyone you want for twenty-five dollars." You could tell her a time to call your boss, landlord, or ex-whatever, and she would come up with an inventory of insults that cut to the bone. The response was colossal—but no one wanted to pay. One guy wanted a date and she wrote back, "Who exactly are you asking out on a date, asshole?" The listing said nothing about her gender or sexuality. I thought her response to him was a good calling card for her work, but he didn't end up hiring her.

In L.A. there's what you say you do, and then what you do. Kind of like the Catholic Church, there's the official and the unofficial word. Officially I'm a director/actor/producer/designer/fill in the blank, but unofficially I'm a waitress/stylist/wedding singer/sandwich guy/fill in the blank. I'm the kind of director who takes the budget shuttle, not the limo.

You can only exaggerate so far. Eventually they see what you drive and it's all over.

Recently, I started teaching a friend of mine to drive at the Hollywood Forever Cemetery, where people drive—not much, but a wee bit—slower. We crept by the Cadillac-sized tombstones with famous faces etched into granite lined by remunerative palms. Flowers from strangers line the graves; there's no love like the love for a stranger. Eventually we reached the back end of the cemetery and found a more humble section, where the tombstones sit like crooked little dog teeth. "This must be where the B actors get buried," my friend said.

"Well," I responded, "I guess they made it in, huh?"

MY MEMORY AND WITNESS

LIS GOLDSCHMIDT AND DEAN SPADE

Dean—

Hey. How's things in NYC? Tired here. Just home from hanging out with everyone. Feeling really tired of the class stuff we were talking about the other day. Tired of people fronting like they're poor or grew up poor or whatever—like it's cool to be poor. You know the deal. They put it on like an accessory. You know? Just like co-opting any culture. Do you know what I mean? It's like people who wear "native garb" from wherever they're exoticizing at the moment—but the thing is, they take it off when it gets old to them.

I guess I'm just feeling pretty pissed. Like I can't take it off. Like it is old. It's always been old. And makes me feel old and fucking tired. And small.

I don't mean to rant.

The main reason I'm writing is 'cause you carry the facts and I feel like I need them. You know the details that I think can help me not feel erased by these kinds of nights. You know how much Mom made. You know the welfare info. It sounds dumb—I know what it was like, but I've spent my whole life pretending it was something else, my whole life trying to pass as something else—and I need the numbers to feel justified or some shit. I need those numbers to prove me wrong or call me out or something. Does that sound weird? It's like I've even convinced myself . . . also like I want some fact to separate me from those people.

I mean I remember it. I remember what it was like. I remember the shame and all that. I remember that greedy excited fucked-up feeling I got when she'd bring home the groceries. I remember swallowing myself one zillion times. I remember being an invisible eyesore. I remember knowing this couldn't be right. When I think of it now I get that same empty, gagging thing. I remember that heavy fucking cloud that hung around our tiny house. That fog that made it so hard to breathe. That stress that kept us all quiet and angry and sad. Remember?

I'm scrambling to think of something good and light, but it goes back as far as I can remember. It only got darker and heavier.

The end was the worst, right? I guess for me it was the worst because I felt like I was the mom when she was sick. You know? Not that we didn't both have to pick up what she couldn't carry anymore. But I remember doing the grocery shopping by myself. You know, I think it's really only the last maybe five years that I don't have some crazy fear while in line at the grocery store. I think this is actually the first time I've really thought about it. There's the shame of shopping at the discount store. Scared someone from school would see us or something—and scared that if anyone ever came to our house (not that they ever did), they'd see the bags from there. (Not to mention just seeing the house!) But then there were all the times we had to put stuff back—do you remember that? I cringe thinking about it now. It was terrible. Embarrassing. I remember being scared to look at Mom in that moment. How she'd look it all over and have to decide what to put back. How did she do that? How can you decide what food your three kids *don't* need? Can you imagine how stressful that must have been for her? *Ugh.* It fucking makes me want to puke. Then there was the shame of using food stamps. It's funny how kids I know now use food stamps with so much pride.

Dean, this sucks. I hate thinking about this stuff. I'm trying to reclaim it or something but sometimes it just feels like Mom trained us so well that passing is easier and the shame is too thick. Sometimes I think I'd make the world's greatest spy because I can pretend so well. Time to sleep.

I hope you're well—

I'm glad we have each other in this.

xo, Lis

Dear Lis,

I took this letter with me to Montreal where I was showing the film Tara and I are making about trans people and bathrooms. While I was there, friends of friends had a "white trash"–themed barbecue. The people I was staying with called the hosts to voice our protest to this theme, and heard that others were also upset, so we went anyway, thinking people wouldn't participate in the theme and that the message had gotten across. Of course, we were too optimistic. Many people came fake-pregnant, with giant Budweiser cans, fake southern accents, and severe blue eye shadow. What to do? I thought about how "trashy" it is for poor people to have children, how differently poor people's substance abuse is surveyed and punished, how easily these white people employed a term that suggests that all nonwhite people are trash while only some white people require such labeling. I thought about the time you were invited to a white-trash event where people were encouraged to black out their teeth, and I thought of how Mom lived her whole life hiding that she had dentures—like everyone in her family—from a time when "dental care for the poor" was pulling out all their teeth in adolescence. When she died I learned she had hidden this from me (you too?) my whole life—sleeping in uncomfortable dentures all those nights during our thirteen years together when I was too scared to sleep alone—all to hide from even me her poverty and shame. (Meanwhile I dreamt of the braces the other kids at school could afford.) I thought of my own consciousness, starting in elementary school, of the need to separate myself from the term "white trash." Be careful how you smell, who sees your house. Try to get Mom not to curse or smoke in front of other people's parents.

But at this party I bit my tongue and turned my head when they arrived in costumes. Couldn't bring myself to speak on this rooftop full of people I had just met. I spend sixty to eighty hours a week exclusively talking about poverty and advocating for poor people, but I could not advocate for myself, could not give up the small amount of passing, of blending in. We left fast and Pascal, Brianna, and I ranted on the street, wondering how we should have handled it, talking about how girl–social conditioning still operates in our trans bodies, convincing us we shouldn't confront. With every passing hour I've become more irate. No place to put it. More anger to add to the churning crushing pile that lives behind my sternum.

> I'm tired of helping rich people appease the guilt about their hoarding lifestyles so they can act a little.

Tired. I hear you about being tired. I'm tired of being diplomatic about poverty. Tired of trying to convince rich people at nonprofits, rich people at foundations, and rich gay people especially to care about and support the lives of low-income intersex and trans people. I'm tired of helping them notice that we exist, trying not to make them too uncomfortable to give money to the struggle that (when we win, which we will) will end wealth and poverty for everyone. Tired of being gentle and nonthreatening and helping them appease the guilt about their hoarding lifestyles so they can act a little. And I'm tired of hearing that you're getting paid less than the private-college educated man who sits next to you doing the same job, and tired of seeing all my trans friends without jobs or adequate housing and trapped in the criminal-injustice system. I'm tired of other poverty lawyers (from upper-class backgrounds) telling me I don't pay myself enough when I make twice what Mom supported four people on in the years she had jobs, and when our clients are fighting like hell for a couple hundred bucks a month from welfare or ten bucks to make a call from jail. I have to figure out how to not get too tired. Sometimes I think that's what killed our mom. Somehow, you and I got out of there, out of that dirty house, off those gravel roads, out of Virginia, but she didn't make it.

I think all the time of what it would be like if she could see us now—if I could make her a fancy dinner in my apartment (artichokes) and take her to see something city-beautiful; if, for her birthday, we could fly her to San Francisco and all three of us could have tea in your kitchen and walk around Golden Gate Park and she'd tell us the names of all the flowers. It's almost Mother's Day.

You asked for the facts. I carry them around like the chip on my shoulder. The most she ever made was $18,000 one year. Our welfare was less than $400 a month. We got a total of $50 when we three spent Saturdays cleaning the glass and mirror store, less when we cleaned houses. The social security survivors benefits our foster parents got for us were about $500 a month each until we turned eighteen. (It's sick that she could support us better by dying but there was not money to help keep her alive.) The jacket she always wanted when she was in middle and high school, that all the other kids had but she never got, cost $7.02 Canadian. The most important fact, maybe, is that if we'd been in the same situation after the 1996 welfare cuts, we wouldn't have been entitled to the same benefits because of her immigration status, and, in my estimation, we would have had a much harder time keeping a place to live or staying together as a family as long as we did.

I love you, Lis. You're my memory and my witness, and my only connection to all that we've lost. I love that you keep the sweatpants Mom got in rehab and that I slept in when you were caring for me after my chest surgery. When I'm not biting my tongue, it's because I'm thinking of how quickly you call people on their shit, how vicious your wit can be, and how you always have my back.

Love, Dean

AUNT MARION, WHO LIVED IN FLORIDA

LIZ MCGLINCHEY KING

WE DIDN'T KNOW ANYTHING ABOUT CLASS WHERE I GREW UP. IN SOUTH-west Philadelphia in the '50s and '60s, we knew there were really rich people in the world, and really poor people, and that we were somewhere in between. If someone were to ask, I guess we would've said we were middle class. But no one asked because we were all pretty much the same. I was well into my twenties when I realized that, with few exceptions, the families in the neighborhood of my youth were working class. Now, in my sixties, my knowledge of class structure in America gives me a more refined description. Although our pride kept us from even thinking we were at all deprived, I know how my family's status back then would be defined today. We were the working poor.

While most families in our neighborhood had more than a few children, we had a few more, with seven kids in our little row house. Dad's salary as a foreman at the carbon factory got stretched pretty thin, barely making it from one payday to the next. Mom managed to serve up three square meals a day, without fail, but her struggle to make ends meet was difficult and sometimes painful to watch. I remember between-meal hunger and what that felt like, but we rarely asked Mom for a snack, because looking in her eyes when she had to say "no" was too hard. A peanut butter sandwich in the afternoon could mean someone would not get a sandwich for lunch the next day.

I had some struggles particular to being the only girl in the house. Clothes for my six brothers were handed down from the oldest to the youngest. My clothes came from brown paper bags discretely handed to my Mom over the back fence. The former owners of my attire, girls on the block who were slightly older than me, never intentionally made me feel bad about wearing their hand-me-downs. But I saw the look of recognition on their faces when I showed up for a game of double Dutch in something one of them wore the summer before. I heard the quiet of the kind moment when they decided not to say anything.

I used to daydream about things being different, imagining what my life would be like with fewer kids in the house. Considering each brother one at a time, I would think about a life with just one of them. Maybe we could dine in a restaurant, something we did not do, not even once, during my childhood. We would have more space in the house. My bed could be moved from its location in a corner of my parents' bedroom, next to the baby's crib, to a room of my own. The third bedroom would be for my only brother. The fantasy ended when I had to choose a brother.

I HAD A CHILDHOOD FASCINATION WITH STORIES ABOUT PEOPLE who moved away. When the girl next door got married at eighteen and moved to Iowa with her new husband, I wanted to know why.

"Why did Eleanor and Johnny move to Iowa?" I asked my mom.

"Eleanor has an uncle there who can give Johnny a good job. He wants to give Eleanor more than he could here, working as a grease monkey," she told me.

I knew he worked at a local garage fixing cars, but I didn't know why Mom called him a grease monkey. I never saw Johnny looking anything but handsome and spiffy clean, because a man always washed up and changed out of his work clothes before coming home.

I especially loved to hear stories about the one member of my family who had moved away—Aunt Marion, who lived in Florida.

Aunt Marion was the older of my mother's two sisters, and stories about her were always told with humor and a bad girl bent. There was the story from her very early teens, when she would take her baby sister out for a stroll on summer evenings to give their mother a break. The walk from their row house in 1930s South Philly happened to pass the Philadelphia Navy Yard.

"We were cruising for sailors!" she would later tell us laughing, during one of her rare visits home from Tampa. And there was the story of how she named that little sister.

"This baby is too pretty to be called Agnes. I'm calling her Dolly." More than eighty years later, Agnes is still affectionately called Aunt Dolly.

There is an old picture of Marion as a preteen sporting a short boy-cut when it was downright defiant for a girl to cut off her long hair.

"Oh, she was a real flapper," Mom told us, while we looked at old pictures around the dining room table.

Marion's choice of living in Tampa seemed like a natural part of her singular spirit. The distance made her mysterious and romantic, even in a trailer park setting. I was well into my teens when I got curious about it. During my daily evening chore of setting the table while Mom prepared dinner, I asked her why Aunt Marion lived in Florida. Mom was standing and stirring something in a mixing bowl—the bowl tucked under her left arm, a wooden spoon in her right hand. She stopped stirring, looked me in the eye and matter-of-factly answered my question.

She told me about the murder.

"Your Uncle Ed came home from work and found your Aunt Marion in bed with another man, so he shot him." I was silently shocked, but Mom was so calm about telling me that I accepted her simple explanation, and never asked her about it again.

Turns out, it was much more complicated.

Here's what I gleaned recently from clippings my sister-in-law and fellow writer, Denise A. McGlinchey, found in the newspaper archives at the main library of Philadelphia.

"Husband Shoots Escort Bringing His Wife Home, Wounds Him Seriously After Scuffle in Chester House." So stated *The Evening Bulletin* on December 13, 1946. Ed, whose age is stated as thirty-three, and Marion, listed as age twenty-seven, lived in the low-income housing projects in Chester, on the outskirts of Southwest Philadelphia. (In true Aunt Marion style, she knocked two years off her age.) They had four children whose ages at the time of the shooting ranged from four to twelve. The children were often left alone while Aunt Marion and Uncle Ed hung out, separately, at local bars. The gas and electric services were turned off for lack of payment. The house had no heat and no lights.

My cousin Elsie was the oldest of their children. As an adult, she did talk about those days and nights when Aunt Marion and Uncle Ed left the kids on their own. Elsie would go door-to-door begging for food, without appearing to do so. Even in the projects, families considered begging beneath them. Elsie would knock on one neighbor's door with her well-rehearsed inquiry.

"My mother said may we please borrow four slices of bread." Then the next door.

"My mother said may we please borrow four slices of baloney." And the next.

"My mother said may we please borrow four slices of bread." Dinner was ready. Baloney sandwiches for four.

Elsie would knock on one neighbor's door with her well-rehearsed inquiry.

"My mother said may we please borrow four slices of bread." Then the next door.

"My mother said may we please borrow four slices of baloney." And the next.

As much as Elsie loved telling a good story, she never talked about the murder. Details remained hidden behind veiled references, to be dug up decades later from media archives.

Further statements from the newspapers: "In his first version of the shooting, police said Klock told them he came down the stairs after being awakened when his wife and escort entered the house. . . . He came down the steps into the unlighted living room—the gas and electricity were turned off . . . 'I saw a shadowy figure . . . I thought he was putting his hand in his pocket to get a revolver. I fired at the shadow.'"

But in an earlier statement, "Klock said his wife grabbed him by the hair while [the victim] beat him . . . Klock said he picked up a baseball bat, hit [victim] and broke out of his grip. The shooting followed."

Headlines from *The Evening Bulletin*:

DECEMBER 14, 1946:

"Woman in Shooting Free. Case of
Mrs. Klock to Be Taken Over by
Juvenile Court."

DECEMBER 23, 1946:

"Woman's Escort, Shot by Her Husband, Dies.
Chester Man Faces Rearrest on Charge of Murder."

MARCH 26, 1947:

"Killer of Wife's Escort Is Freed.
Chester Man Cleared Speedily by Jury."

Uncle Ed not only got off on self-defense, he got sole custody of the children, who had been relegated to a local Catholic orphanage. That's when Aunt Marion left her hometown and started a new life as the only person I ever knew, "Aunt Marion, who lives in Florida."

IN THE SUMMER OF 1958, WHEN I WAS SEVEN YEARS OLD, I heard my mother and grandmother talking about Marion coming up from Florida to spend the summer. She had decided on Atlantic City, New Jersey, for her summer stay. She would be close enough to the family to easily visit, but not too close to cramp her independent style. She was coming north to procure a divorce from Uncle Ed, having lived apart from him for ten years.

My aunt settled into her Atlantic City life. She found a two-room apartment, got a job at a local diner, and reestablished a bond with her kids, by then in their teens and twenties. She sometimes borrowed a car and drove across the Walt Whitman Bridge to visit us on Sundays. She was full of stories that made us laugh, like the one about her parakeet that cussed.

"My parakeet can say, 'son-of-a-bitch' and 'goddam it!'"

If there was no cold beer in our house, she used the Ladies Entrance at the Irish Pub on the corner and came home with two quarts. One summer Sunday, she proposed an idea to my mom.

"Let me take a couple of the kids back to Atlantic City with me for a week."

Mom, having given birth to my youngest brother less than a year prior, never passed up the opportunity to farm out a couple of kids, and Marion's troubles, except for her affinity for beer, seemed to be long past. So off I went with my next oldest brother, Mike, to spend a week in Atlantic City. No one thought to ask what she would do with us when she waitressed every day. Mom was just happy to have fewer kids to feed and watch after, even if only for a week.

Aunt Marion left for the diner every day around noon. She told Mike and me to be quiet and not disturb the neighbors and when she got home she would take us to the boardwalk. Marion always kept her promise of a walk on the great Atlantic City boardwalk. But some of her troubled behavior was still in the works.

One evening I was using the bathroom and discovered there was no toilet paper. Aunt Marion left to go to the store, leaving me on the toilet. She got sidetracked and stopped for a beer, or two, and it was quite some time that I sat there waiting for the toilet paper. Mike talked to me through the door, pushing funny objects through the inch of space between the bottom of the door and the floor to keep me entertained. I saw a safety pin, a roll of Tums, and a salt water taffy. Finally the door opened and Marion handed me a roll.

Another day, she and the landlord got into a loud, outdoor argument because he claimed her lease didn't allow for children and she told him she'd invite, "whoever the hell I goddam well please," and started knocking on the neighbors' doors inviting people to her apartment. It was the most fun Mike and I ever had packed into one week.

We could hardly wait to get back to school and write our What I Did on My Summer Vacation compositions.

At the end of the summer Aunt Marion's business in the area was complete and she returned to Florida. She and the family had bonded again, and Marion would make a trip from Florida to see us every couple of years or so. She was no longer a funny story told around the dinner table. She was a real and permanent part of our lives.

It would be several years before I learned about the family murder, but it didn't change who she was to me. Until her death in 1991, she was one of the most beloved members of our family, and hands down the most colorful. As Aunt Dolly puts it, "My sister brought her problems on herself. But she was always the most generous person I knew. She didn't have much, but christenings, first communions, and weddings never passed without a gift. She would give you the shirt off her back."

I often thought of Aunt Marion when I was a young adult, sharing an apartment with two women in West Philly and barely getting by. I remember mornings at my first job when I drank whole glasses of milk by the office refrigerator, milk that was meant for coffee. More often than not, I got to work on payday after handing the trolley driver my last thirty-five cents. At times when I felt the financial stress and hunger pangs of adult life with no one to call to borrow a buck, I thought about Aunt Marion, and how she lost everything, albeit by her own hand. Nevertheless, she picked herself up, replanted herself, and just kept going.

In 1994, in a covert act she would approve, the family hid our aunt's box of ashes in our grandmother's coffin for a bargain burial.

Today, more than a hundred years after she was born, family gatherings rarely take place without a story or two about Aunt Marion. She is never talked about as the aunt whose husband killed her lover. She's Aunt Marion, who lived in Florida.

WINGS

tatiana de la tierra

PLACING A PINK-FEATHER HEADBAND IN MY HAND, MY ABUELA BLANCA kissed me goodbye, crying. I cried, too. I didn't know why. The perpetually gray Bogotá skies joined in, sprinkling us with cold rain. I ran up the narrow metal staircase as wind bit my wet cheeks, into an airplane that would take me and my family far from Colombia. It was May 1968 and I had just turned seven years old.

Thick, warm Atlantic air greeted us as we clambered, wide-eyed, out of our metal cocoon. The air in Miami was nothing like the air I knew in the Andean mountains. But being yanked from the love and protection of my aunts, grandmothers, and great-aunts was the most momentous change. It was bigger than air itself. I walked to the market with them, chit-chatted on the sidewalk, made corn arepas at the crack of dawn, collected eggs in the morning, accompanied them in the evening for hot chocolate. They cooked for me, bought dresses for me, introduced me to all their friends. But in Miami, everybody was a stranger.

At the airport I played with stairs that moved and doors that opened magically. A strange twig of a man who wore ripped denim and spoke halting Spanish greeted us. "*Yo aquí para ayudarte*," he said, offering a warm handshake. Harvey was a friend of a friend of my dad's; they embraced as if they already knew each other. My mom looked at him cautiously through her reddened eyes. Finally, she extended her hand.

Everything seemed brand-new and shiny those first few days. All the blades of grass were uniformly green and stood properly on plush manicured lawns. The clean-shaven policemen wore immaculate starched uniforms and drove sleek cars crowned with little blue and red domes that sometimes flashed and made wailing noises. Neat rows of containers housing exotic foods filled the spotless stores, where clerks counted crisp bills over Formica counters and gave back the change without stealing. Exquisite paintings graced cereal boxes and cans of soup, and luminous rays emanated from curvy Coca-Cola bottles branded with fire-red labels.

My father took me to a 7-Eleven, where I marveled at the cans decorated with vivid color images of the foods they contained.

"This one, Papi," I said. We both scrutinized the can. It had a picture of reddish brown beans on the label. Beans, a mainstay of our diet, had to be soaked in water the night before and took hours to cook. Yet here they were in the palm of our hand, ready to eat. We went home with the can. My father opened it and heated up the beans with some rice. I could tell they were different; they were watery and didn't smell right. Still, I brought a spoonful to my mouth. I gagged as the flavor hit my palate. They were sweet. Beans were supposed to be salty and spiced with onions, garlic, tomato, and peppers. They were supposed to be thickened with green plantains. They were not supposed to be sweet or watery.

My mom, who disliked cooking and had little time for it, took advantage of the cheap and instant foods. She went grocery shopping and came home with Kool-Aid, white bread, processed cheese, frozen chicken potpies, sugar-coated cereals, and Hamburger Helper. The Colombian foods I was accustomed to—fresh blackberry juice, farmer's cheese, Creole potatoes, tamales, and empanadas—quickly became memories.

But my dad's hunger for familiar foods roared incessantly. He enjoyed eating and cooking, and he went to great lengths to find magical ingredients. He discovered that you could find fresh coconut milk in the shell, ripe guanabanas, cumin powder, and plantains in bodeguitas like La Ideal and Los Pinareños. You could get an entire meal—a bandeja paisa with real arepas—at La Fonda, a Colombian restaurant. One day, my father took the bus and went foraging, his eyes bulging with visions of Colombian food. He returned late in the afternoon, his shirt splattered with drops of sancocho, his breath greasy from fried empanadas, his belly expanded with sobrebarriga, his fingers sticky with dulce de leche. He was beaming. He brought us avocados, coconuts, yucca, plantains, and Colombian delicacies.

On Saturdays we took the bus to Miami Beach and went swimming by the pier, on the southern tip. There, I dug my toes into the sand and bobbed in the salty ocean. My mom, who was pregnant, sat on the beach and read a book while the rest of us played in the water. We ate peanut-butter-and-jelly sandwiches and drank Kool-Aid. Once, as a treat, we went to Kentucky Fried Chicken after being at the beach all day. They had a special offer—two pieces of chicken with a biscuit and a small Styrofoam cup of mashed potatoes and gravy for $1.29. We got a special and sat down to share the food. I bit into a drumstick. It was good, crunchy and spicy. But as I swallowed I recalled what had happened the day before we left for Miami, and my stomach became queasy.

We were in El Libano, at my great-aunt's house. It was our last day there. I was in the corridor that faced the garden when I saw that Cuki, my favorite chicken, was being hunted down. "Run, Cuki, run!" I screamed as I saw a shiny machete swinging in her direction. I gripped the wooden porch railing as she ran, headless, fluttering her golden brown wings in a futile attempt to levitate. Cuki, who used to peck at my feet when I showered on the patio beneath blue skies, was our last supper. I missed her, and I missed the black earth that caked my feet when I played in my great-aunt's garden.

Our first home in our new world was a room in Harvey's house. Blond, blue-eyed, and eccentric, Harvey slept on the beach, washed dishes for a living, and drank rainwater that he collected in an oxidized metal container in the back yard. He nourished himself on tropical concoctions, blending whole papayas with fish guts and honey. Restaurant napkins for toilet paper and roadside-discarded produce for dinner were his gifts. He taught my mom to walk on the grass to extend the life of shoe soles. He came home every few days to drink the rainwater, wash up, and change clothes. Harvey didn't believe in pesticides so roaches crawled freely on the walls—and on us. He didn't believe in banks or the government, either. His living-room library was stocked with books about politics, anthropology, and history. He let us live in his house for free, until we could afford to rent a place on our own.

Another Colombian family soon joined us, moving into the room across the hall. The coziness of our home disappeared with the violent intrusion of our new neighbors. José Miguel was my dad's military companion from Colombia. He was a construction worker, thick and muscular, who wore a constant snarl on his face and stank of liquor. His wife, Irma, took care of us while my parents worked. One day, my mom came home earlier than expected. My brother and sister and I were cowering in our room as José Miguel beat Irma. Their little girls, Nubia and Cacallo, were screaming throughout the house. My mom grabbed a broomstick and busted in on him. "*Béstia!*" she yelled, leading a sobbing Irma into our room.

> We walked around the neighborhood together, marveling at the gringo houses and the gringo lawns and the gringo postman and the gringo talk.

The scenes repeated like tired reruns. When José Miguel wasn't home we were free to run and play, but as soon as we heard his boots step into the house, we froze. "¡*Chito!*" we warned one another, walking on tiptoes, trying to be invisible.

But not everything was bad, because I was with my brother, Gustavo Alberto, and my sister, Claudia. They were my only friends. The three of us walked around the neighborhood together, marveling at the gringo houses and the gringo lawns and the gringo postman and the gringo talk. Gone were the mountains that ringed Bogotá, the matriarchs in the countryside, the gamines who begged for money on the street, the fresh air. We didn't understand why we had left Colombia or what the future held for us. So we did what we knew how to do, no matter where we were. We played. We ran and kicked bottles, climbed trees, played tag. We dueled as cowboys and Indians. I wore my pink-feather headband and protected my tribe. My brother brandished his miniature machete. My sister was the village elder, scheming to outwit the troops.

In August, three months after our arrival, my little sister was born. Natasha came home in a white wicker crib that my mom had bought used for $1.50. Cushioned with a new white satin pad and lined with blankets, pink balloons floating on the flannel, the crib wobbled on uneven legs. Natasha, who was conceived in Colombia, was the only U.S. citizen in my family. She was a real gringa and even had golden hair. She was my life-size doll. I changed her diapers, prepared her bottles, and cradled her in my arms.

My childhood had come to a close. Summer was ending and school was about to start. Irma found a job and couldn't take care of us anymore. My mom worked as a maid in the Tudor Hotel in Miami Beach and my dad worked in a paper factory. I was the oldest, so my responsibilities increased. I began to cook, clean, and take care of my siblings. I became a miniature adult. "Wash that plate!" I scolded. "Clean up that mess!" I nagged. But I never got the response to my commands that I expected.

If we hadn't left Bogotá I would still have been wearing my gray uniform to school and learning to pray the rosary. I would have come home to my mom and played outside and done my homework and had *arroz con lentejas* for dinner. I would have been a seven-year-old girl just like all the others. But Bogotá grew more distant every day. After four months in Miami it seemed that we were there for good.

School was an enclosed city surrounded by banyan trees and hibiscus bushes where I became indoctrinated into another culture. Gimnasio Palestina, my first grade school in Bogotá, was a private school in a small brick building. But Shadow Lawn Elementary took up an entire block. It was made of concrete and had dozens of classrooms, a cafeteria, a gymnasium, and a playground. In Bogotá my school had one class and one teacher, but in Miami there were hundreds of students, many teachers, and a principal. I was the only light-skinned girl in my class and one of the few Spanish-speakers in the entire school. I couldn't speak English and was just beginning to understand some of the words.

I sat in silence at my desk with a thick pad of baby-blue-lined paper and a yellow No. 2 pencil that had been given to me for free on the first day of school. Mrs. Clara sent students to the chalkboard to write words that she dictated. She called on me; I stood at the front, looking at my feet, frozen. She read her list: ocean, river, stream. I fingered the chalk and she repeated the words, eventually chanting them as if they were commands. "Ocean! River! Stream!" I didn't even attempt to write on the board; I went back to my desk, my fingertips dusted with white chalk.

I dreaded those public moments that highlighted the fact that I was a foreigner. Sometimes I sat at my desk plotting my revenge. I would master the English language. I would infiltrate the gringo culture without letting on that I was a traitor. I would battle in their tongue and make them stumble. I would cut out their souls and leave them on the shore to be pecked on by vultures.

One pivotal afternoon, I squirmed in my seat. I had an itch between my legs like a red-hot ant bite. Finally, I reached my hand toward the ceiling to ask for permission to go to the bathroom. Mrs. Clara looked at me; I knew no words to express my state of emergency. I pointed to the door; she stared back blankly. The whole class looked on. I grabbed my crotch, squeezed and grimaced. Finally, she understood, but as I darted out of the room, warm pee exploded between my legs, trickling into my socks and splashing in droplets on the floor. I ran out of school, my moist shoes pounding on the speckled tile, squeaky drumbeats echoing in the corridor.

Past the banyan tree by the playground and through the neighboring streets, I sprinted as if I were being pursued. I ran with the insides of my legs soiled, wet, and sticky with urine, sucking oxygen into my bursting lungs with wrenching gulps. I wished that the stiff metal airplane that had ripped me from my home would take me back. Pumping my arms, I wished for silver angel wings that glided or long, broad eagle wings that soared. But I knew that my flapping was useless.

THERE ARE HOLES IN MY MANDARIN DOG BISCUIT

SHELL FEIJO

THE STRETCH OF MY FAVORITE SHIRT AS I PULLED IT OVER MY STILL-DAMP hair helped ease me into the day ahead. Going to school had never been easy and middle school at MLK had proved to be no exception. The teasing had begun almost as soon as I climbed onto the bus for the first time. Words like "greasy," "dirty," "smelly," "pizza face," "poor," "trash," "welfare case," and so on engulfed me on a daily basis. But, I had found friends and muddled through, making jokes at my own expense until the teasing subsided. After all, the rest of the kids on the bus weren't much different. They were probably just using me to get the focus off of their own clothes, smells, lives.

Anyway, I smiled that morning getting dressed—I always felt good when the red-and-white-striped T-shirt that I loved fell snug against my chest. As I turned to leave, my mother reached out and grabbed my shoulder, saying, "You aren't wearing that, there's a hole in it."

I pulled away. "Everything I have has something wrong with it. This is my favorite."

"I don't give a shit. You are not wearing a shirt with a hole in it."

I started to cry. I ran back to my room, grabbed a dirty sweatshirt, and yanked it on, tears streaking down my face. I ran down the six flights of stairs and out into the sweet stench of a Berkeley morning, hoping I wouldn't miss the bus and have to walk.

I thought about the hole in the shirt a lot that day, as though I were wishing the shirt back into its pre-hole existence, the worn-in comfort that it had had the day we bought it at the thrift store. I felt empty without the T-shirt holding me tight, cold without its striped warmth. When I wore it I imagined there was no pain, no queasiness, no hunger. But soon the shirt was forgotten; more pressing issues were at hand.

Rushing home after school, my stomach would groan and shift, crying out with after-school hunger pangs and butterflies of hope that my mother would not be home when I got there. I climbed the stairs, silently praying that when I rounded the dark hallway I would see the outline of a note, taped glistening to the door. When it was there, it meant going in and sighing with relief, making a baked potato when we had a bag, or getting a cup of the sugarless cheap drink that nobody else's mom made them drink. My mom had to be the hippie welfare mom, no Kool-Aid or Skippy peanut butter here. Only chunks of natural peanuts in a layer of oil, and pure, juice-flavored water. Some days, I would rush home and in note-inspired bliss I would wander the apartment, imagining that my mom would never come home, never yell again, never hit, never cry, never stare at me with the hurt of her whole life transferring to me, through me. Other days, the hunger would be too much, and I would search the kitchen, thinking maybe I had missed some small piece of cheese, or a leftover piece of chicken in the fridge. Never had anything been overlooked, but there was always the box on top of the fridge.

No matter how much we struggled to stretch the food stamps or the social security check my mom got for being legally blind, mentally ill, and unemployed, the dog always had bones.

It never failed that no matter how poor we were, how much we struggled to stretch the food stamps or the social security check my mom got for being legally blind, mentally ill, and unemployed, the dog, the beautiful Doberman my mom had gotten for protection, always had bones. Purina dog biscuits, at that.

The first time, I tried them at my mother's demand. She said there was nothing for dinner that night, and that dog biscuits were really made out of "people food."

"Really," she said, "they have more nutrients than anything I would cook. If you are that hungry, eat one." Dog biscuits taste like crunchy box. No flavor, just crunch, and a mealiness that makes you feel full even when you have tasted nothing of any substance. I guess they must taste different to dogs. But, they weren't so bad. They weren't like rancid meat or anything, more like a really healthy granola bar from the overpriced natural food co-op around the corner.

The taste of the dog biscuits was better than the acid pinch of memory that comes to me as a mandarin orange. Mandarin oranges and I go way back. Back to the couple of months we lived in Albany, in the rented house with the fat tree in the yard. The house with roaches crawling under the kitchen sink and over the walls when the dark descended at night. The house where the electricity got shut off. The house where my mom and her latest boyfriend smoked and snorted, stayed in bed all day and yelled all night. The house where a sleepover turned into torture, all on account of those damn mandarin oranges.

MY BEST FRIEND, NIKKI, HAD COME ON THE BART TRAIN ALONE, all the way from Concord. We had overnight plans of giggling and reading together, snacking and sipping ice-cold Coke late into the night, covering up the glare of low-battery-flickering flashlights with torn blankets and just the right angle of bodily shield. Nikki was the only friend I would ever invite over, the only one who could be trusted with my secrets, the only one I had ever known with secrets of her own. The night of the mandarin oranges is the last night I remember us together. Maybe she was scared to come back. Maybe my secrets had proved to be too deep.

We were hungry and there was nothing to eat. I don't mean that there was only peanut butter and jelly, or milk instead of juice; I don't mean that there was nothing we liked. I mean there was nothing there. I walked down the hall apprehensively, the familiar butterflies grinding against my stomach, and knocked quietly on my mom's bedroom door. She answered in her nightgown. I told her we were hungry and asked if she had any money for us to go to the store.

Clutching the five-dollar bill with delight, I chased after Nikki, screaming that I would catch her as we approached the nearby Lucky's. We slowed to a fast walk, sweat pooling with kid-funk on us as we laughed and entered the shiny mecca of food. We struggled past the potato-chip aisle and stole peeks at the bakery cookies. We had my mom's last five, and a TV dinner apiece was what we were allowed to get. I chose the veal parmigiana, a 99-cent favorite, and Nikki picked the Salisbury steak meal. We held hands and waited to check out in the express lane.

I know I had the five. I had been holding it so tight I could still feel its crinkle, its damp presence in my palm. The checker glared at me and said, "Do you have the money or not?" I started to panic and could feel tears welling up. Nikki tried to help, and took off through the store's aisles, scanning for the wrinkled bill. After an eternity standing there and the realization that the money was gone, I asked the checker to hold the dinners while we searched on the street. We walked back and forth in a crisscross pattern, without saying a word. I was supposed to bring back the change—the three dollars left over—and dinner for Nikki and me.

Finally, we gave up. It was very dark and my tears had turned to sobbing. Nikki let me lean on her and we slowly edged home, so different from the girls who had bounded toward the store. I turned the knob slowly and tried to sneak in. My mom was waiting. She was mad. "Where have you been? It's been over an hour."

I started to tell her that I was sorry. I wanted her to know that I really didn't mean to lose the money. I said, "Mom, I don't know what happened. I was holding the money real tight but when I went to pay, it was gone." Whack! She slapped me hard, and turned to Nikki. "What did you two buy?"

"Nothing," Nikki said. "We picked frozen dinners and then the money was gone." My mom took my arm and dragged me into the kitchen. "Well," she said, "now you are going to eat what I fix. The last of my cigarette money." She mumbled for a while, slamming empty cabinets and cursing. Nikki stood transfixed, wedged into the corner of the kitchen, staring at my mom.

"Come here," my mom said. "Get in line."

Nikki stood behind me and my mom opened a large can, placing it in front of me with one fork. "Take turns eating one bite at a time, and finish the whole thing. This is your dinner." I tried to swallow, but the tanginess stung my tongue and the crying had made my throat tighten. I didn't even feel hungry anymore. I started to spit and my mom yelled, "Oh, no, you wanted dinner, you lost the last of my money, you are going to eat." Nikki stepped in front of me and grabbed the fork, taking a huge bite. The liquid sprayed, making my face sticky, and Nikki reached for another section of orange. I think she was trying to save me from eating it. My mom pushed her out of the way and told me to eat up.

I tried again, and this time the force of the fork plunged against my gag reflex, and I threw up everywhere. My mom paused. For a moment, I thought she was going to make me eat it. Instead, she said, "You girls have had dinner. Now clean this shit up and get to bed."

We cleaned late into the night and fell asleep from sheer exhaustion. We never did play that night, tell stories, or giggle. We fell asleep listening to the sounds of each other's growling bellies, and woke to my mom thanking her boyfriend for a bag of food. We ate cereal that morning, and cold milk. No one ever mentioned the canned mandarin oranges.

LOCKED IN MY MIND IS A MIST OF CHILDHOOD EXPERIENCES LIKE this one. They run together—food, clothes, pets, houses, fights, family—intertwined with one another, flowing and stopping as they wish, resisting separation into neat categories. These childhood experiences all revolve around money, and the lack thereof. As I reflect on them now, twenty years later, they boil down to one memory, an amalgam that reminds me, that speaks to me, that scares me: There are holes in my mandarin dog biscuit.

ON EXCESS

CHLOE CALDWELL

HAVING EXTRA TOILET PAPER INSTANTLY MAKES ME FEEL LIKE I AM ON vacation in Hawaii. I've never been on vacation in Hawaii, but you understand what I mean. Extra toilet paper is relaxing and clear and luminous, like I imagine Hawaii to be.

Having toilet paper is the opposite of shaking out your vagina and hoping for the best, or walking like a penguin to the kitchen to see if there are paper towels (there aren't, of course there aren't), or using napkins stolen from a bagel you got to-go three weeks ago.

Having toilet paper is not having to use the scratchy cardboard toilet paper roll to wipe yourself, because that's better than using nothing, or is it?

The bathroom in our house growing up did not have a closet. No cabinet holding boxes of name-brand tampons and towels and lotions. I didn't care, it was the toilet paper I coveted. I wanted to use a whole handful, all at once.

THE VACATIONS WE TOOK WHEN I WAS A KID CONSISTED OF CAMPING with little cereal boxes. We went to Assateague Island and I returned covered in angry mosquito bites. The other kids in my class came back tan from The Bahamas with heads full of braids tied with hot-pink and turquoise beads. I didn't know what "The Bahamas" were but I knew we wouldn't be going there. My friends would send me postcards with photos of beaches on them. *Wish you were here!*

Neither of my parents had college degrees. My father was a carpenter, buying tools on credit cards from Sears, running his own business before his knees got bad in 1997 and he opened a musical instrument store. We didn't have health insurance until my mom went to work at a Head Start preschool for low-income families.

My parents didn't have money but they were not stupid and knew there were ways of providing education and teaching creativity to their kids—you don't need money to walk in the woods, swim in a creek, pick flowers, or read. I feel eternally grateful for this and realize it's why I became a writer; money wasn't my ultimate goal because I knew you could be fulfilled without it. I am thankful I had nothing because I appreciate everything. I am easily pleased; there is no room to be high maintenance or scrutinize a gift from someone, I am grateful to get anything new, always.

MY MOST FINANCIALLY DIRE YEAR WAS AT AGE TWENTY-SIX. I spent the year without a debit or credit card, only using cash. I cashed my checks from Powell's Books, about $300 every two weeks, at the Fred Meyer grocery store. Then I'd go to the Whole Foods lunch counter where you could put fancy salads into brown boxes and eat the heavy parts (falafel) while standing in line so the price would come to $4.00 instead of $8.00.

I bought miniature travel toothpastes and would pay my rent in cash, then try to resist the serious urge to go steal a $20 back from the stack I left on my landlord's table.

Friends didn't always get it.

"He's the kind of person," I remember a friend saying about her ex-boyfriend during that time, "who puts three dollars of gas into his car at a time."

"Oh yeah," I scoffed along with her, though I did that too. I never filled up my car with a full tank until I was thirty. It made me anxious to spend that much money upfront.

THERE WERE SLIGHTS BY FRIENDS, AND FRIENDS' PARENTS, WHEN I was growing up, cutting comments I didn't always understand then but do now. The way they'd describe my house as "cozy." The way they'd chuckle about our sulfuric tap water. The way buckets were in my room to catch the leaks from the roof. The way our couch had ink and blood stains on the pillows. The way one of my friends told me my neck had dirt on the back of it.

Some of my closest friends had hot tubs and pool tables and bathrooms in their bedrooms. We'd eat foods we didn't eat at my house, and I'd pretend I'd had them before: artichoke hearts, poached salmon, asparagus, edamame, oysters, lobster. I'd watch the others eat until I'd seen how it was done, posing as a slow, relaxed eater, the opposite of what I am. I'd mimic their way of pulling off artichoke leaves and opening edamame pods, all while my body was in a state of anxiety of being found out, not passing, being ostracized, ridiculed.

I always found it uncanny how close the phrase *insufficient funds* is to *insufficient fun.*

HAVING MORE THAN $300 IN MY BANK ACCOUNT GIVES ME THE same feeling of luxury that having extra toilet paper does. I can go to a restaurant and take out my debit card (I can't afford credit cards), slamming it on the table without scrutinizing the bill and worrying about overdrafting.

I always found it uncanny how close the phrase *insufficient funds* is to *insufficient fun*.

Just the words "excess" and "extra" light me up like Times Square. I don't expect extra. I've never asked for extra mayo on a sandwich nor have I had extra bottles of wine or beer in my fridge in case friends dropped by. Wine racks are foreign objects to me; I never fathomed the point of owning anything designed especially for having too much at one time.

This goes for clothing, too. I've asked the salespeople if I could wear clothes out of the store. It's a big hassle, they don't like it, but sometimes I don't have a choice.

I've known people with clothing in their closets with the tags still on them. Trusting them is difficult.

DURING MY TWENTY-SIXTH YEAR, I KNEW I WAS SORT OF MENtally unhealthy and bleak, thanks to poverty, so I went to a free clinic for therapy. I saw a woman with blonde hair that always looked recently brushed, and she told me I could come see her once a week for free if her poodle could stay in my session. I said yes.

Being broke is bartering, taking what you can get, feeling tired all the time, eating a string-cheese while walking around the co-op, hoping no one notices.

It's taking what's available to you.

I take bread from the bread basket at fancy restaurants, Ziploc bags when I'm baby sitting, stamps from jobs.

When I was twenty-five, my boyfriend and I were at Whole Foods, procuring picnic foods. On our way out, I spotted the napkins and utensils for the people who are eating at the store. I went to take two of the metal forks, and two knives.

"Please don't," he said.

I rolled my eyes. "Are you serious?"

"Are *you*?"

I didn't take the forks, but I was miffed, and from then on the disconnect that already existed between us widened.

In my early twenties, I had a friend who would steal from the store Rugby on Fifth Avenue. One day my friend Noelle and I offered to go with her, to steal with her.

"If you don't mind, I'd rather go alone," she told us. "I'm trying to look like I have money."

Having no money is having nothing white. No marshmallow fluff. No white towels. No beds in hotel rooms with comforters and top sheets (which explains my fetish with them now).

White shows dirt, and when your belongings get filthy with stains, you hold on to them anyway.

When I was nineteen I had a twenty-six-year-old boyfriend who bought luxuriously thick toilet paper, twelve-packs at a time. Sometimes I'd go to his place while I knew he was at work so I could shit and use the toilet paper instead of using the thin kind at my own house. I loved taking handfuls of it, more than was necessary.

"I don't know where all my toilet paper goes," he used to say.

Old habits die hard. *Just stole some toilet paper from Rivertown Lodge,* (a high-end hotel where we live in Hudson), I texted my boyfriend a few weeks ago.

Such a you thing to do, he texted back, accepting me as I am.

For the first time in my life, at age thirty-one, I live alone. When I can't afford to go on a fancy tropical Instagram-worthy vacation, I buy a twelve-pack of toilet paper. Just like that, I'm on a beach in The Bahamas, hot-pink beads in my hair, sand between my toes, a margarita in my hand.

THE LOWER-WORKING-CLASS NARRATIVE OF A BLACK CHINESE AMERICAN GIRL

WENDY THOMPSON

I MADE MY LIFE FROM SCRATCH. BUILT THIS TWENTY-TWO-YEAR-OLD BODY from nothing. Just two wires and a burnt-out car, two pieces of tarp, and some scrap metal. And with these I built my bones, my skeleton, and my skin. A home to withstand sleet and rain, drunken assaults, and rape. A space to create beauty and dream, to leave a part of myself behind as artifact.

I came into this life carved out of poverty and half Blackness. Grew up on Lucky Charms and public-access television, I thought, like everybody else. I was cared for by my mother, an immigrant from Burma who shifted from Chinese restaurant waitress jobs to working as a baby sitter. I was punished by a Black father who came home tired and hungry from punching numbers at a shipping company on the Oakland waterfront.

My mother reminded me that it was her idea to wait in line overnight while pregnant with me back in the early '80s to try and get a loan from the bank to buy a house. She asserts (usually implying my father's failures) that without her, our family would be nothing. She wanted to make things work for herself and for her daughter. She needed to prove something to her family after getting kicked out and disowned for "going Black" and shaming the family name.

My African-American father grew up hard. He didn't hustle and was always intent on making money the "honest" way. He still had hope that this white man's world would be just, that they'd cut a little Black boy from San Francisco some slack. But he was angry and could not change the spiral of his own small life and stayed trapped in the menial-labor pool while his white coworkers got the raises and vacation time slots. All he got was some damn sweater with the company logo on it after twenty-plus years of "excellent service."

So this was my beginning, growing up in a lopsided house with my father's burnt-out anger and my mother's shaky dreams. We lived in Oakland between gunshots and freeway overpasses. My parents always had ambitions of making enough money to buy us out of the urban streets. Of course they wanted to give all three of us a nice little house with a picket fence and green grass to hide our abuse and sadness in. Not with nights of barricaded doors because a boy armed with a loaded weapon was loose in the neighborhood. Not with the neighbors across the street hosting gang parties and someone being fatally stabbed in a whirl of music and beer. Not with prostitution and a stabbing on the corner, a vague picture of a Black man being passed around as the suspect.

But this is the compromise—we were not white, we were not rich, we were not privileged. My mother couldn't speak English and my father was trying to swallow the whole of employment discrimination and a new family. In my own world, I was trying to save my skin from getting beaten up by classmates because of the poor Salvation Army clothes I wore or the way my half-breed awkwardness caused them to feel ill at ease. I got driven to the "good school" in the hills because my parents wanted the best for me. Not for me to break down at eleven and start fucking the neighborhood boys, getting drunk, and cutting school with a baby on the way. No, not that.

> My mother wanted me to be a good little Asian daughter; my father wanted me to be able to escape the violence and dejection of growing up Black. They both wanted me to have a "chance" and make it in this world.

My mother wanted me to be a good little Asian daughter; my father wanted me to be able to escape the violence and dejection of growing up Black. They both wanted me to have a "chance" and make it in this world. So my father beat me to make me grow up tall and straight. My mother taught me to stay away from Blackness, to carefully construct myself so that I would not fuck up, and to hold it together until we reached the safety of suburbia and the middle class. Maybe, they thought, the whiteness would rub off on me. Maybe it would save me from cutting my arms with broken glass and running away with drunk homeless boyfriends.

But after all my father's efforts to beat me straight and my mother's insistence that I stop "acting ghetto" (read: an exaggerated performance of what I thought was Black), I ran away anyway. It wasn't the two-story house that I wanted so much, but this was beyond their comprehension.

Poverty and race, then, like stealing napkins from McDonald's for our own kitchen table or buying in bulk when my mother would steal from my father's tight wallet, were one and the same to me. I had grown up half Black and poor and had felt ashamed of myself and where I came from ever since I got thrown into schools with other kids who could afford to buy their social status. Those kids, the ones who were worth being called on, the milky White Rabbit candy–hands raised to a teacher's ambitious question. And the girls—from elementary to high school—always had the luxury of looking pretty, while I had only what I could afford, and even if I could afford it, would it ever be enough?

From this I became the unwanted, dusty half-breed girl from the other side of the tracks. I ate old food wrapped up in aluminum foil for lunch. Stinky food sometimes. Chinese food.

I do not know when I began to relate racism to whiteness, class and poverty to supremacy and economic/corporate tyranny, my family in the bottom of the curved belly of American lies. This kind of consciousness wasn't entirely mine at a young age since I lacked the framework and mental capacity to understand it all, but in the little ways that I could formulate it, I learned that I wielded a power and strength that these little Richie Rich kids would never have. They had all the privilege in the world, all the workings on their side, but I was still standing, still surviving after a thousand-year captivity that their world and their books constantly tried to erase from history, from memory and re-create as myth.

For so long, they—politicians, pastors, teachers, the three-car-garage rich—pushed the "pull yourself up by your bootstraps" theory. They said, "You Black people are so lazy. If you got off welfare and worked hard, maybe you could make something of yourselves in life."

But we Black people have been making something of ourselves in life, not only for ourselves but also for white people, for generations.

They never seem to hear us, though.

BEING HALF BLACK MEANS HAVING THICKER BLOOD AND BONES to withstand breaking, and eyes with a raw, wide-open perspective. (Not all of us choose to live or see, but those of us who do know the difficulties of staying on top and navigating the currents of life.) Being poor is knowing how to make old milk and some bread go pretty far over the course of a week. Being a woman is learning from a young age what you can get in return for sex. So, my mother fed me on what she could make work, and what I didn't get from my parents, I received in exchange for my body, for all I was worth. And it isn't worth too much in this society, Blackness in the female form. Especially when you have to eat and have no skills, or are underage. *Blame it on history.*

For me, being half Black, poor, and troublesome somehow took the crime out of my rape and battery. It wasn't necessarily a legal issue that a young woman from *that side* was out in the streets getting beat up because she refused to give sex without some compensation. It wasn't a crime that she was being neglected in her home, it wasn't a crime that she went into the streets to look for an alternate family system. In that respect, I became a statistic, a government-study number, what talk-show hosts might call "a troubled girl looking for a father figure and love." But it wasn't severe enough for intervention when a young, poor woman who was labeled "gifted" by teachers in school but "mentally unstable" by psychiatrists was being battered and seeking alternatives—but found too many bricks instead that, in the end, created dead-end walls.

Still, I was literate. I loved English and my Anatomy class, even. And I stuck through school and graduated. During that time, I kept in my company a transient boyfriend who was also mixed-race but looked white, the same one who did the majority of the assaults on my body. My liberation came when he went away to boot camp the summer after senior year. At eighteen I was referred, as a "bright and qualified student," to college, and began yet another adjustment at the University of California at Santa Barbara, the U.C. notorious for being unable to keep students of color at the institution. It was a four-year fraternity party from which I bailed after just two years because of severe depression, alienation, and a climax of threatening to knuckle up with some of the white girls who constantly harassed me in the dorms.

I was not the first in my extended family to go away to college, but coming from an immediate family with a Chinese mother with minimal English skills and an African-American father who went to a city college and hit the glass ceiling hard, my attending a four-year university was not some minor thing. I transferred schools, determined to complete my bachelor's degree, unfinished with the fight.

I was still recovering from the earlier abuse, physical and mental, from boyfriends and other men. I was still trying to find my space to surface and not drown in academia, a place I was not totally prepared for after so many years in the California public school system, where I was channeled into underachieving classes because the school had already filled their "quota" for the honors courses. I was still cutting up my body periodically as my own way of coping, and would sometimes go out drinking to forget my difficulties. When I did study, I had to beg to borrow other kids' books because if I spent my financial aid money on the textbooks for my courses, I wouldn't be able to buy a Greyhound ticket back home to visit my family for the holidays.

I endured financially in school by depending on loans and painful budgeting. Even now, nothing for me is ever a luxury. I learned to stretch money and sometimes starve because something else is always much more important than food, something else always comes first. It's the sacrifice I have learned to live with while my mother supports the two younger additions to our family—two more girls—on minimum wage earned as a cashier at a fast-food restaurant. I used to be very ashamed to admit to people where she worked. Admitting these personal things can still remind me of the hurt I felt growing up poor and being made fun of.

It's our (brown) bodies that this society was built on and is still being built on, our backs, our hands still in the dirt. And it's easy for someone from outside this "class" to discredit the everyday struggle, simple for them to dissociate themselves from our shame, our labor, our humility, our anger. My mother has never been ashamed of who she is, even after her Chinese relatives cussed her out for going with a "nigger" and having half-breed babies without being able to support them. She fought to stand firm with her choices and stay proud of her work—owning a home and a car, helping one kid through college with two more to go. But what she does is regarded by American society as "nothing," a dirty shit job: mopping up someone else's floor and taking in their shame; probably even serving from a drive-through window some of the people who will read this book. Same as the work done by my father—refilling paper clips, photocopying papers, running Post-it note messages to court superiors—a "go get my coffee, boy." No one seems to notice that my parents, two underprivileged people, are doing the body work, the labor that keeps part of this world functioning.

Some of us survive, even as the world is caving in on us under the spread of capitalism and global industry. Some of us find new ways to pay the rent, pull together a family in a one-bedroom apartment, pay for an education with hope that a back will be spared—and hands too—while dealing with the persisting circumstances of poverty. There is a desire to close the gap between privileged and poor in this country, but it seems that regardless of the amount or quality of labor performed, the demarcations remain. The borders between the upper class and the working class stand to define more than just the amount on a paycheck. They classify language, culture, body, and self. It keeps us apart from one another while also keeping us connected in a never-ending struggle for social and economic balance. The middle ground is where I locate myself.

THE SOUND OF POVERTY

EILEEN MYLES

WHEN I THINK ABOUT THE TYPE OF POVERTY I GREW UP WITH I'M INCLINED to call it "enough." We had just enough. I guess we were what they call now the working poor. We weren't really poor, but my parents were afraid of that—poverty. So there were many actions and choices in between us and poverty and we lived in that in-between place where you were always slightly reminded that you didn't have enough or you had barely enough.

I always think of the powdered milk. What kid didn't like to drink milk, tons of it—a half gallon was plunked down on the table at supper and at lunch. But sometimes my mother sank down a pitcher and there were tiny bubbles at the top of it and we'd scream: No, Mom, it has bubbles. It's powdered! It's not, she'd insist. Then she'd give in. O.K., she'd admit. It's half and half. Everything was always getting stretched a little bit. At a moment when everyone was proudly aware of the pop glamour of American products, we didn't use Welch's grape jelly—we used Ann Page, the A&P brand. Or Finast from First National. When it came to ice cream it was Marvel, whatever that was, and it was also neapolitan so that nobody could have their favorite flavor, everybody could have striped ice cream or nothing. Neapolitan is strawberry, vanilla, and chocolate. You probably know that. We didn't have Kool-Aid, we had Cheeri-ade, our supermarket's brand. I loved when we ran out of something just before supper because I'd jump on my bike and go to the Monument market in the center which was run by some Italian guy who wore a straw hat and the Monument only carried brand names, we were locked in to something known. But usually we weren't. As a result, there were certain things that actually seemed disgusting to me. Like butter. Too rich. I preferred margarine. I had to develop a taste for butter in college so that I wouldn't embarrass myself by my preference for blandness. I'm afraid to taste margarine now because I think I would still like it too much and I would think about home. Growing up poor—growing up anything other than middle class situates you strangely in the culture. For instance, I don't like television. Unlike every middle-class girlfriend I've ever had, I watched it plenty growing up. No one ever stopped me. Also, it was the sixties. TV was like a national sport. Those people who were questioning whether it was good for kids were total outsiders. Conceited and rich. Probably the same people who were willing to put their entire family on TV, like the Louds. My family would eat supper and then my mother would make about three dozen chocolate-chip cookies and we'd watch TV until it went off. We'd watch Johnny Carson and then we'd watch American jets fly over Buddhist temples and "The Star Spangled Banner" would play and we'd call it a day. Nobody did homework. Nobody asked. There was no future.

Nobody did homework. Nobody asked. My brother was considered a brain and he got good grades somehow and I didn't but it didn't matter, because I was a girl.

We were just there. My brother was considered a brain and he got good grades somehow and I didn't but it didn't matter, because I was a girl. So right from the beginning it seemed that being female was another occasion of poverty. In fact there were two of us in my family. We were referred to as "the girls." Immediately I was part of a group. It's been pointed out to me that in photography kids of color are generally photographed in groups rather than in individual portraits like white kids. In general, it seems to me, girls are less white than boys, or white in the wrong way. And again, there were two of us, so the more, the worse. And I was more a part of the group of my family than the group at school. My family was kind of Old-World. If all the females were getting permanents, I would get a permanent. There was no personal self, no point of resistance. Whatever style was tearing through the legions of other girls at school had no effect on the fashions of my family. Since there were two girls we would often get the same thing: two dresses, identical. My brother was a little different from us. There was the sense that he would go to a brand-name college, and my mother helped him buy a car in high school—a Volkswagen; yet still in the most basic ways he was just like us. He watched TV and he went to bed. He got up and the jelly and the margarine were there and—let me show you our lunch boxes. It was cool to have your sandwich on a big bulky roll—but of course instead I had Wonder Bread—oddly one of the brands that broke through to the working class. Everyone had it. I think Wonder Bread was considered good because of all those ways it built the body and it was also great to have a Drake's cake in your lunch box, but I did not have a Drake's cake, I had an apple with a bruise. It's better for you, my mother would defend it. And she was right. But still I couldn't believe those lucky kids would open their boxes or their bags and a product in cellophane would gleam out at them. And they would tear it open and the whipped cream would be stuck to the paper and it was theirs.

IN SCHOOL THERE WAS A BAND. I DREAMED ABOUT IT—A MARCHING band with drums and clarinets and saxophones—the best. I desperately wanted to join the band and play music with everyone. But my mother simply said no. We couldn't afford it. My brother had a paper route so he could afford it, but Terry didn't practice. Why would my mother waste the money on a horn I wouldn't play, she explained snootily. She actually had distaste for the idea. But I would, I believed, my hopes fading into the wallpapered walls of our two-family house that we owned. See, we weren't poor. We were World War II white average. My parents bought our house on the G.I. bill. Obviously other guys went to college on it as well. Not my father. My father decided to drink himself to death and die instead. When we wanted something my mother would immediately compare her experience—orphan, to our experience—lucky ducks with two parents, and then even one. It was easy to say no to me. She would think of what she had had—what they had taken away from her. At the point at which both of her parents died, there was a pianola in her house and she believed it was hers and the Polish relatives came and carted it away. People take everything. That's what my mother believed. I think we kids were "people" too. By the time I was eleven and had given up the possibility of ever playing the trumpet, or the clarinet or the saxophone, and merely sat on a chair in the parlor tooting on my harmonica, my mother would lean in and say, You know, I always wanted to play the piano when I was a child. She looked at me sadly. We were a couple of kids. So it's really difficult when I think about growing up without money, not much of it anyhow—to figure out what in fact was the weirdness of our exact economic situation and what was the kind of mourning that people endlessly express through dollars. My mother couldn't let me replace her loss with a living kid with a horn. I had to stay empty too. And I did. I really think of language as a replacement for everything. Sitting here at my computer it's like the revenge of nothing. I make my constant claim in silence. I toot my horn.

GHETTO FABULOUS

TINA FAKHRID-DEEN

BUYING A HOUSE IN THE 'HOOD WAS A SOCIOPOLITICAL DECISION FOR ME and my husband. I didn't want us to be the type of Black folks who get a little money and flee to the suburbs, away from our people. I live in Chicago. I was born on the west side of one of the most segregated cities in the nation, in the Jane Addams projects, a place commonly referred to as "the ghetto." It was a few miles west of downtown and close to everything imaginable—a prime location.

My family was poor, but resilient. We were no strangers to food stamps, roaches, and hallways that smelled of urine. We often had to eat those black-and-white-labeled generic brands and drink powdered milk, which I despised. I learned early on that sugar on a slice of bread or mixed with a glass of water made a tasty afternoon snack when peanut butter and jelly or Kool-Aid were unavailable.

I am proud of my roots and my complex identity, so it makes me sick when I hear people speak negatively about the ghetto, the place that I called home for many years. It is common to hear white and Black middle-class teens, in a skewed attempt to embrace hip-hop culture, say offensive things like, "Oh, my God, he is acting so ghetto," or, "Look at my big ghetto booty." Although the word "ghetto" refers to a section of the city densely populated by a certain minority group and was formerly where all Jewish people were dumped in some Eastern European countries (and later in Chicago and other big, American cities as well), the term is used quite differently now.

To those on the outside looking in, the term "ghetto" is now synonymous with being Black, dirty, attitudinal, ignorant, lazy, uneducated, and dangerous; it has taken on the same connotations that the term "nigger" historically has had. However different, they are both politically loaded terms used to denigrate poor Blacks, but to acknowledge that would be politically incorrect. "Ghetto" is the new code word for "low-income Black person." Whites won't acknowledge it because it feels too close to being racist, and middle-class Blacks won't acknowledge it because in their hearts, they know that using the word is a sad attempt to distance themselves from the lower class, to assimilate and be accepted by mainstream culture. It would be a public admission that poor Blacks are reduced to frightening caricatures, misunderstood by the majority of American society, still overtly oppressed.

I am ghetto. I love hip-hop, Ice Cube, and the Geto Boys. I have a big butt and snap my neck back and forth when I'm cussing someone out. I look good in cornrows and wild afros. I can do the "booty" dances with the best of them and I still say "ain't" to get my point across. I also have good parents, who always encouraged me to be the best and to speak my mind. As a result, I have a master's degree in education. No, my mama is not on welfare and yes, my father was present while I was growing up. I've never committed a crime, unless you count the time I stole a piece of bubble gum from 7-Eleven and returned it two minutes later out of guilt. I have a beautiful husband, not a "baby daddy." I've traveled to at least six different countries, studied abroad, and wear "ethnic" thrift-store dresses to work. I plan to teach our child Spanish and sign language. My ghetto identity is more than the latest booty-shake video, it is my foundation, and it reverberates through every facet of me—textured and rich. And no, I am not the exception.

My old neighborhood was ghetto. The scent of month-old chicken grease filled most homes, and stained blinds hung in the place of flowery curtains. There were scattered winos on the sidewalks, glass shards on the playground instead of wood chips, rampant petty crime, graffiti on the walls, and boarded-up windows on some apartments. There were also community centers where we could go and play board games and get juice and a "choke" sandwich (so damn dry you could choke eating them) until our parents got home. Hard-working parents worked several jobs to make ends meet and to provide a good, loving home for their families.

In school, we had spelling bees and learned Spanish in kindergarten. Caring adults with knowing eyes watched over us if our parents weren't around. We all knew one another's names and who to call when a child got out of line in the street. We were a community. My friends were ghetto. We did ghetto things, like drinking buttermilk with cookies and mixing Kool-Aid with sugar, giggling at the sour-sweet taste in our red-stained mouths. We played double dutch with a long extension cord while singing "take a peach, take a plum." Each time the jump rope hit one of us in the face, we had bitter fistfights, wind-milling with our eyes closed, hoping to make contact. At Halloween, we got yelled at or whipped for throwing eggs, not because it was childish and rude, but because we were screwing with the food supply. Some of us grew up to be construction workers, accountants, and teachers, while others became gang affiliates, hood rats, and drug dealers. Some moved out of the projects; some remain to this day. Some went off to college; others went off to prison. Regardless, we all shared the same history, cried the same tears, and mirrored the same struggle—withstanding poverty.

My family moved away from the projects when I was about six. We lived in the suburbs and then down South for a brief stint, but moved back to an urban area on the North Side of Chicago marked by many of the same characteristics as my former ghetto. Basically, we were still poor and struggling to survive. Upon returning to Chicago from college, I searched the city for housing. I drove back to my old neighborhood and, to my chagrin, found most of it had been torn down—shiny new town homes with skater boys stood in its place. It was now called "University Village," because a local university had bought up most of the property. Even the hospital where many of my friends and I were born had disappeared without a trace. It was almost as if we had never existed. It made my blood boil that all of those poor people had been displaced, and I wondered where they had gone. I blamed middle-class America and greedy developers. I accused the mayor and his cronies of turning a blind eye to what was happening in poor communities like mine.

I wanted to live in a place where all socioeconomic backgrounds were represented, no one above the other. I finally decided to move back to the North Side, for the diversity in ethnicities, cultures, and economic status. The local fruit market sold everything from *kimchi* and plantains to yucca and collard greens. *Elote* carts rolled down the street with hot ears of corn as often as ice cream trucks. Blue-collar and white-collar workers rode the el train together each morning. There were little coffee shops on several corners, adorned near the entrances by the occasional evening prostitute or homeless man. In my building lived a Jamaican drug dealer who often threw wild parties with the scent of cheeba oozing under the door; an alcoholic white man and his six-foot grocery cart–toting girlfriend, who fought like Ali and Frazier in a title bout; a spiritual Black vegetarian who swore that a cat's purr meant that it was going to attack her; a wiry ballerina who rented out her place every other month; some Eastern Europeans who spoke little English and managed the building; me and my mathematician husband; and an interracial couple who just seemed shady.

Slowly, many of the buildings in our area were converted to condos, the asking prices beyond ridiculous. The poor were being forced to move out, just like in my old neighborhood. They left a few Section Eight homes intact, for nostalgia's sake. Although gentrification came rapidly to our neighborhood, we weren't directly impacted until my mother (who lived down the street from us) was forced to move out of her tiny one-bedroom apartment when her rent jumped from $475 to

$1,250 a month. Then our building changed hands, and the new owner threatened to almost double the rent for our modest one-bedroom. We all needed to move, and fast. My mother purchased her first home on the far South Side. Loving the diversity of the North Side, my husband and I tried to find another local property to purchase, but the price hikes were happening everywhere. We considered the suburbs, but quickly came back to reality. Why buy into the reverse white flight and allow upper-class whites to move back into the comforts and convenience of the city while we got stuck out in the boondocks, disconnected from everything we knew? So we did the most intelligent thing we could think of, we invested in Bronzeville, a historic South Side community.

DURING THE GREAT MIGRATION OF THE EARLY 1900S, MANY Blacks emigrated from the South in hopes of landing industrial jobs in Chicago. Bronzeville was one of the only areas of the city that southern Blacks were allowed to live in. It is legendary for its sizzling-hot blues scene and notorious 47th St., a strip of juke joints, jazz cafes, restaurants, and hotels. This is where famous Black artists such as Billie Holiday and Ella Fitzgerald came to perform and stay when they had a gig in town. For years after its heyday, Bronzeville had been a poverty-stricken area filled with crime, despair, and little development. This was now one of the hot spots in the city to move to, because of its accessibility to downtown and the lakefront, and its affordable housing.

In a matter of days, we found a beautiful three-bedroom condo with a monthly mortgage in the same price bracket as our old apartment's rent increase. Set right on the main boulevard—named after a well-known Black civil rights leader—we could see all types of Black people walking up and down the street. This was the first time that I had been back in an all-Black area since my days in the ghetto and the South. It was exciting and wonderful, although I did miss the ethnic diversity of the North Side. There was a new Black-owned poetry cafe and a bank, and the alderwoman's office was less than a block away. It was rumored that a comedy club, performing arts theater, art gallery, and bookstore were in development on the next corner. Across the street, a sign boasted a new town-home development starting at $350,000. My husband and I thought that our neighbors were fabulous and incredibly nice. We had two lesbian pastors across the hall, three outgoing drug dealers, otherwise known as "pharmaceutical representatives," two PhD's, an ex-cop, a lawyer, and several high-powered businesswomen. We were all so close that it was like living in the dorms again.

I soon realized that I had somehow crossed over and was officially middle class. It was confusing, because I wasn't like the bourgeois Blacks who knew nothing about hard times and mocked the accursed lot of poor folks. I was different. I cared about civil rights for everyone. I didn't turn my nose up at the thought of eating pig feet or chitlins. I didn't fear that my property value would go down because poor folks lived next door. And I didn't refer to all less fortunate people, especially the expressive or thuggish-looking ones, as "ghetto." Then my whole reality changed. Within a week of our moving in to our new building there were two attempted robberies. I was four months pregnant and actually heard them kicking in my neighbor's door. A few weeks later, someone's car was broken into; then more robbery attempts in the coming months. I began to fear coming home late in the evening. As a pregnant woman in her third trimester, I was truly defenseless. My mind began betraying me. I questioned whether this neighborhood was good enough—safe enough—for me and my family. I feared the possibility of my child picking up broken crack vials in the neighborhood park during our afternoon strolls. I thought about sending our daughter to the substandard neighborhood schools. I thought about someone actually getting into our home, violating us and everything we've worked so hard for. I thought about moving—moving far away from crime, far away from my present reality, and even farther away from the ghetto we now lived in. It no longer felt like home—it felt like prison. It felt dangerous. It felt unforgiving. I felt like I was being punished for leaving the 'hood and coming back with a pot to piss in. I saw jealous eyes ogle me as I entered our six-foot gate, making sure it slammed behind me. I became resentful, fighting rage. I felt like a traitor.

I had become that middle-class asshole who moves in and pushes aside the poor residents, who are rightfully angry. They wanted the good life too.

I had become that middle-class asshole who moves in and pushes aside the poor residents, who are rightfully angry. They wanted the good life too. They wanted big-screen TVs and Jacuzzis like us. They wanted to feel important and respected, as we did. They also craved quality community resources for their families. No matter how I tried to frame it, I had become one of the powerful pawns in this gentrification game, with the poorest of Bronzeville being knocked clear off the board. Like magic, with our middle-class presence, the schools would begin to get better, more commercial development would find its way to the area, and politicians and policemen would make special visits to our condo association meetings to hear our concerns. We would complain about the crime and beg for the removal of it, of "them." My sensitivity for the wretched poor would wear thin. Ill feelings would grow between us and "them" until someone gave in and moved on. There could be no coexistence between the classes. We misunderstood and distrusted each other too much. There could be no community here.

Not until we stop to realize that we're all in this together. Not until I use my newfound middle-class power to advocate for the right to decent and affordable living for my new neighbors, here in Bronzeville. Not until I help them to advocate for themselves. Not until I realize that some of these residents don't want or need our middle-class handouts because they were doing just fine before we got here. Not until I understand that many of these families are just like mine was back in the day, working hard and trying to keep food on the table. Not until I treat them as equals. Not until I stop being scared and open my mouth to say "hello" to the skeptical faces that eye me daily. Not until I recognize that the ones trying to rob us are just lost souls with no hope or heart left (that doesn't mean I won't keep calling the cops). Not until I get the resentment out of my heart.

The ghetto is a community filled with ups and downs, struggles and survivors and people sticking around hoping that things will get better. Being ghetto is so much more than a new catchphrase or a hip-hop song; it's an identity, a reflection of our economy, and a way of life. Just as hip-hop will be in my blood and spirit forever, so will the ghetto. I will transcend the box that us ghetto folks have been put into and create a new space. I will make people think before using the term "ghetto" to refer to any person, place, or thing. I will fight for the right to be ghetto, even when my back's against the wall, being violated by those I'm trying to stand up for. That's keeping it real—real ghetto. As a people, when one of us suffers, we all suffer. In my heart, I know that we ain't a true community until we take an honest look at one another and begin to embrace every part of our intricately woven culture. Black folks must get a handle on the crabs-in-a-barrel syndrome, and learn to stand strong, together.

GETTING OUT

FRANCES VARIAN

FEAR TASTES LIKE METAL ON THE BACK OF MY TONGUE. IT SITS HEAVY ON my rib cage, making it difficult to breathe. A thousand small pinches beneath my skin. One hundred bells ringing in my skull at the same time. Fear is my sun and I orbit around it.

> The only way to get money is to work for it and there are only two kinds of work: smart or hard.

And everyone I was born to orbits in the solar system of the punch-clock. There was never a time when my face wasn't turned toward something greater than myself. Fear and poverty breed shame. Exhaustion and disappointment make everything taste bitter. The tired body cannot convince the racing mind to sleep. The sun will rise. Then we will work. These are things you know instinctively. Without money bad things will happen to you and you won't be able to stop them. The only way to get money is to work for it and there are only two kinds of work: smart or hard. You enter the world, pull for air, and wait for payday.

I don't want to write about class. To write about class is to pull a carefully placed bandage from a wound and poke at it. What are my choices? I can romance you with stories of working-class pride and sacrifice. I can tug at your heartstrings with tales of desperation and injustice. I can show you my scars. I can try to describe the rage. I can tell you what it feels like to be the daughter of a janitor. I can tell you what it feels like to be a graduate of Vassar College. I can tell you how to simulate a blowjob over the phone for strangers. But after I am done telling you all of these necessary things I still won't have any money. And I will still be afraid. So what are my choices?

Here's how my Roman Catholic Polish family likes to play a game I call Wheel of Getting the Fuck Out of Here. It's a game that most working-class people play on some level. First, everyone has a really screwed-up childhood with abusive, alcoholic parents. Then everyone finds their own partners and makes babies. (In the Polish Catholic version, the babies must come after a proper Catholic wedding.) The most important thing to know about Wheel of Getting the Fuck Out of Here is that you, the Player, will never get the fuck out of here. The only one who can possibly get out is that baby you just made. Your job is to move the Game Piece (baby) around the board so that she is able to "work smart." If she works smart, she will make money. When she has money, she will not be so afraid. In order to move the Game Piece you must work so hard you cannot remember your middle name. You must spin the wheel to see if your dead dreams can be reincarnated in your child. And most important, you must teach your baby the importance of getting out. You must hold yourself up to her time and time again as inspiration to flee.

I am a wayward Game Piece, maybe a design flaw. In this particular game the Players (my parents) did most everything correctly. They worked and sacrificed and buried their dreams. They did everything they possibly could to make sure they won this game. They had no idea that the object of their struggles would grow up to reject it just as she was on the verge of getting the fuck out. If they craved a life easier lived, they would not experience it through me.

When I was still a child, we drove past the most spectacular group of buildings near our home in upstate New York. It was Vassar College. My parents said it was a school for rich girls. They said Jackie Kennedy went to Vassar. I thought it looked mysterious and beautiful, like castles. (I would later learn the term Gothic as it applies to architecture and black lipstick.) I wanted to be there so much I could taste it above the fear and I said, "I'm going to Vassar just like Jackie Kennedy."

And that's kind of what I did: I went to Vassar. I just did it a little differently than the former First Lady. Upon hearing my childish declaration, my father quit one of his two full-time jobs and obtained a position at the college as a security guard. He had learned that if he was an employee of the college his child's tuition would be waived, providing his kid could get accepted. I was not yet in middle school.

My father was born in 1927. I was not born until he was forty-nine years old and he has no other children. He is a charming man. Handsomely rugged in appearance and quiet, he is almost immediately likeable. He's towed cars, been a courier, a school-bus driver, a janitor, a security guard, and many other miscellaneous things. He has worked at least two full-time jobs, more than eighty hours every week, for at least forty years. He was gone often when I was growing up and was frequently exhausted when he came back home. My dad's work meant he was on his feet, cleaning, lifting, moving, and protecting, almost all the time. He is still, at seventy-six years old, part of the invisible fleet of people who keep our bathrooms clean and our mountain bikes from being stolen. Kept invisible because who among us wants to look at the stranger cleaning our shit off of public toilets? His is a life dedicated to the service of thousands who will never know his name.

My father adores me. I often suspect it was the combination of his enormous strength and endurance and his devotion to the women in his life that led me to love butches and tranny-bois as an adult. It was for me he played Wheel of Getting the Fuck Out of Here like no one had ever played before. This is the romance I warned you about.

I would come to learn, as a student, that tuition remission was considered a perk for professors and their families. It was not unusual for the child of a faculty member to apply to

Vassar. But in 1994, the kids of security guards came knocking only slightly more frequently than they had in Jackie Kennedy's day. It left me with an out-of-place feeling that wasn't necessarily unpleasant but that has remained with me ever since.

None of that mattered when I entered Vassar. The castles, the ghosts, all of the people with nothing better to do than take their brains out on long walks enchanted me. We were doing work. It wasn't lazy to sit around all day and read—it was mandatory. I took whatever crumbling faith I had remaining in the Catholic Church and placed my bet on humanism. I was going to become a scholar committed to the pursuit of knowledge and I was going to work smart. Vassar was powerful enough to catapult me so far out I would never have to look back again. My first week of school, dozens of kids stomped around complaining because they hadn't gotten accepted into Brown. I had no idea what "Brown" was.

This experience, I imagine, is similar to that of other working-class kids who are the first in their family to go to college, or a certain type of college. My entire life thus far had been a battle strategy to get me to this place. Everyone's resources were used in this endeavor and now I was on my own to navigate the Seven Sisters experience. The rules, language, and vantage point of the upper class are different from mine. They know very little about the lives of working-class and poor people. I watched professors from one of the most liberal colleges in the United States walk past my father like he was a polite ghost. Perhaps we are only interesting in theory.

Throughout my freshman year, the majority of my friends on campus were cleaning ladies, security guards, and cafeteria workers. They were the army who made it possible for me to study feminist film theory, *Othello*, and the elements of moral philosophy. I was, unequivocally, the safest person on campus. My bathroom was the cleanest. My meals were often free. I was their collective darling. They were watching someone on the verge of getting out and they guarded me as something precious.

I loved school. I loved spending entire Sundays in the enormous stone library with its secret passages, stained glass, and ghosts. I knew the information I had at hand was powerful because it was so well hidden. The library was for members of the Vassar community only. And of that community, only faculty and students made use of the resource. Staff cleaned and guarded the building, but they did not check out books very often.

The better I understood my education, the angrier I became that most working-class and poor people are denied one. Why are the children of doctors, lawyers, and engineers taught the mysteries of existence while the children of janitors and waitresses are taught fear? I developed a preoccupation with my own inadequacies, aided by a few professors of elitism. To combat my growing anxiety, I began to envision myself a class spy. I would soak up all of the information they could give me and run reconnaissance for my team.

With time I began to question the validity of Wheel of Getting the Fuck Out of Here, which felt very much like questioning the existence of the sun. If I was so close to getting out, why was I still afraid? Why did I want to leave the people who had been so good to me? The reality of my upper-class peers was so drastically different from my own—did I really want to become exactly like them? And even if I wanted to, I knew it would be impossible. I could make millions of dollars and I would still wake up every morning searching for something greater than myself. I could transform myself into the most sophisticated intellect and they would still be able to smell my fear.

There exist the wealthy and the working class. At Vassar I learned the two are not mutually exclusive. No matter how rich I might become, I will always be the daughter of a janitor. I will always look the woman who empties my garbage in the face. I will always say thank you to the man who serves me lunch. I am one of them, and I do not want to Get Out unless they can come too.

That was it for me, the Game Piece. I would not take a lucrative corporate job and I would not participate in the brain drain of the working class. Game Over. The culture of the people I come from is as valuable as any I have studied. Our language, our unique perspectives, our strengths and weaknesses deserve critical attention. It is not our status as workers that prevents our happiness, but the glaring and obscene disparity between our paychecks and the paychecks of the ruling class. Working-class culture is not something we should run from even if we are offered the opportunity to escape poverty.

Poverty is not a natural conclusion. It is an invention. We are not poor because we are inferior as a group of people; we are poor because it is imperative to the global economy that a limitless supply of labor exist. The labor must be cheap and disposable.

This Game Piece respectfully declines the opportunity to exploit the labor of somebody else's mother or father. As long as we believe it is desirable to get out of the working class, we will continue to be afraid. Assimilation does not free us; it whitewashes the most obvious lie ever told. The Game is a con. The Wheel is fixed. It's time to invent a new one.

What are our choices?

FIGHTING

BEE LAVENDER

THE FIRST FIGHT I REMEMBER, I WAS FIVE YEARS OLD. MY UNCLE ANTON had just married a dimpled, dark-haired girl; the church was filled with golden light streaming into my eyes, and I blinked jealously from the front row. The girl had not asked me to be in the wedding.

After the ceremony there was a cake reception in the basement of the church and my family stayed on one side of the big drafty room, sitting on folding chairs behind round folding tables. The bride's family stayed on the other side—except for the maid of honor, the bride's little sister, Susie, who had been sneaking drinks from some old man. She went from table to table in her cotton eyelet dress with yellow bows, giggling and talking to people. Susie had dark hair cut short like Dorothy Hamill's, a bowl shape on top of her head. I watched her moving around the room and wished I could have that hair, but my straggly reddish blonde hair was past my shoulders and my mother set it each night on squishy pink curlers. In the morning she combed out the curls and sprayed on hair-spray. My hair fuzzed in soft curls for a few hours and then fell straight again before the middle of the day.

The flower girls were all from the bride's family, little girls in eyelet and ribbons, and I didn't want to talk to them. My Aunt Louisa held my hand and walked me over to the strange girls and introduced us. "These are your new cousins," she said. I didn't get it; why did I need new cousins? I had so many already, we were related to most of the town. The little girls stared back at me. They were wearing cute white bonnets with yellow ribbons under the chin; real brown curls trickled from under the bonnets and all the way to their waists. They didn't say hello; they just stared. Apparently they didn't need a new cousin either. Aunt Louisa let go of my hand, patted me on the back, and walked away to talk to Susie. I turned and walked away from the girls. They looked mean.

The church party broke up quickly, all the presents were loaded into a truck, and the bride and groom made out in front of the car my dad and some of the other grown-ups had decorated with shaving cream and tin cans tied on with string.

Back at my grandparents' farm, the real party started, with just our family and the neighbors and a few of the teenage friends of the teenage married couple. The uncles had stacked cases of Budweiser on the back porch, and Grandma Vi had cooked a big dinner of macaroni noodles and tomato sauce with crumbled hamburger, store-bought greasy whole chick-ens, and packages of flaky pull-apart rolls.

My mother brought in plates of deviled eggs, which had been stored in our trunk during the wedding, and she stood in the kitchen laughing and talking to her sisters as she mixed up tuna to spread on tiny pieces of sliced rye bread. My mother was beautiful, young; she would have been twenty-three when that party happened. She was wearing a green velvet dress with puffy sleeves. All seven kids in her family started blonde and ended up dark, like the relatives from Finland—dark-haired blue-eyed people with high cheekbones, everyone with broad shoulders, the women with soft breasts and curving hips, a good place to sit if you were small enough to demand the privilege. I wasn't that small anymore, but I was small enough, and my mother loved me and held me tight. I could still sit in Grandma Vi's lap, and I could still ask my mother to carry me when I was tired.

I played with my cousins in the sewing room, a white room with a huge closet we used as a fort, a magical portal, and a hiding place, standing between or behind the rows of Grandma Vi's silky polyester dresses, which smelled of acidic perfume, Lysol, dog. The whole house smelled of dog; there was Tuta, which they said meant "girl" in Finnish, a mixed German shepherd with a happy face and waggly body. There was Boyka, which I suppose meant "boy," or was a bad translation or joke or something; he was a big red Irish setter, tall and strong enough that I could ride him like a horse. He was Anton's dog and would go to the new house with the new couple. There was Conrad, a white wolfish dog, rescued by my Uncle Frederick from an abusive home. He was friendly and sweet and known to attack anyone wearing a uniform. There was a tiny, ancient black mop of a dog named Midgie who had always been around and probably dated back to my mother's childhood. Midgie was territorial about Grandma Vi's recliner, wouldn't let us sit in it. She went everywhere we went, and Grandma would buy her ice-cream cones and hamburgers.

We played in the back room and the grown-ups sat around the house, smoking and drinking and cracking jokes at the new couple's expense. We ate off paper plates, the plain red tomato sauce seeping through, bits of food dropping off to be eaten by the dogs. People started going home, the great-aunts first, with their assorted kids and grandkids, then the teenage friends; they had other parties to go to that night. Soon it was mainly family in the house and it was late, and my mother told me to lie down on the couch, then tucked a crocheted brown and red afghan around me. My own little dog snuggled with me on the flat, dirty silk pillow stitched to commemorate a stranger's trip to a foreign port, Manila or Okinawa, the memory fades. I fell asleep listening to my mother and her brothers and sisters, all together, all laughing, Grandma Vi and Grandpa Tom and assorted husbands and wives in the dining room and kitchen.

I woke up to the sound of glass breaking, voices raised in anger. I sat up and hugged my little white dog to me, confused. My mother ran past, coming from the bathroom with towels, and said sharply, "Put on your shoes." Had I done something wrong? What was happening? I reached down for my shiny, black buckle shoes. I slipped one small foot into a shoe and was pushing the strap through the buckle when a roar and a chorus of screams made me look up, just as my uncle, the groom, came running straight at me, face red and mouth cracked open in a hideous scream, his eyes the eyes of a horror-movie maniac. His brother, the one who rescued dogs, was behind him, tattooed arm reaching forward to grab his shirt, ponytail disheveled; Grandpa Tom was there too, his hand on Anton's belt. Anton screamed a conquered-warrior scream, a victim scream, the sound of a sick and dying animal cornered and fighting back. My uncle and grandfather leapt forward at the same time, tackling Anton, and the three bodies hurtled through the air, sliding across the coffee table in front of me, pieces of their errant bodies connecting with my knees, arm, head. They slid across the coffee table and landed in a heap next to the front door, knocking over lamps, and my little dog jumped into the fray, biting at any piece of flesh he could reach.

Someone grabbed me and yanked me off the couch, and it seemed like I was flying through the rooms, carried aloft like lumber, one shoe dangling, the other lost in the fray of fighting men, grunting and pummeling one another. I screamed, "No, no, my puppy!" But whoever was carrying me ignored my screams and ran away from the fight, past the remains of supper on the big oak table, through a kitchen spattered with blood and sparkly broken glass, through the dark porch and outside. I could smell whiskey and beer and then I was standing with no coat in the yard, next to the picnic table and the sandbox, the silver dollar plants and willow tree, the bride.

She was crying, and in the dim light from the nearby chicken coop, I could see mascara streaming down her face and neck, making smudges on her white shirt. We were alone. The rest of the family was inside, and we could hear them yelling, dogs barking; but we had been set aside, sent away into the exile of the yard. My foot with no shoe on was wet from the dew on the grass, the night was cold, and I could see stars and a sliver of moon above the orchard. The bride cried and cried and I patted her arm. "It's O.K.," I said. "This doesn't happen very often."

THE NEXT FIGHT I REMEMBER WAS MY OWN. I WAS SIX YEARS OLD, and I was playing in the woods across from my house, a tangled mass of blackberry bushes and salal and wild rhododendrons, evergreens shading our special places. The children of the neighborhood—not so much a neighborhood, really, just four short streets of low-income housing set down next to an abandoned city dump, on the far southern outskirts of the county—had made paths in and out of the remnants of the forest closest to our homes. We had clearings and we had hollowed logs; there were tiny winding trails and some bigger trails our dads made for dirt bikes. I was in the woods, in a clearing, on a sunny weekend day in the fall, after kindergarten started, before the rainy season.

The two red-headed girls from the yellow house, the only one with an eight-foot fence around the whole yard, were with me, along with my best friend Shanna's younger brother, Todd. Shanna was locked in her house doing chores; she was three years older than me and faced a vastly more complicated system of rules—commensurate with her status as an older kid, a fourth-grader. Todd was two years younger than me, not in school yet, a baby; but a mean-tempered baby with the whitest of white hair, dark suntanned skin, ripped denim jeans, and the top to a set of Underoos worn as a shirt.

We were playing a game where the girls were the pioneers, in wagons, trudging across the deserts and barren plains we had seen on television Westerns. It didn't occur to me then to wonder how the pioneers who went all the way west, to the Northwest, the Olympic Peninsula, the very farthest tip of the United States before it drops into the ocean, covered in a dense, mottled, cold, impenetrable rain forest, had managed their journey. Now it seems to me that the barren plains, though barren, would at least have been easier to walk across. No hacking away at scrub.

Todd was the ox, tied up with a jump rope, pulling our weary pioneer wagon as we sang songs and worried about ambush. "Faster, oxen," I called to him, tapping his bottom with the wooden handle of the jump rope. Laura and Jeanne giggled and Todd said it would take more than that to make him go faster. I tapped his bottom harder, and he stared at me with his cold baby eyes. "Is that all you can do?" he challenged me. I tapped again, harder. He laughed at me and the girls giggled. "How about this?" I asked, and hit harder. He kept laughing. I raised my arm above the soft bottom he was wiggling at me, daring me, and brought the wooden handle down with a *thwack!*

Suddenly the "ox" reared up, ropes swinging in an arc, and he wasn't a pretend animal anymore but a real one. He shoved me to the ground and pinned me, hitting and scratching as I pushed and writhed and tried to get away. The red-headed girls had stopped giggling and were standing there with their mouths open, and then they ran away, not to get help, but to hide behind their high fence. I shoved at Todd but I was shocked and scared, and he was a solid boy.

We rolled in the dirt and then he had his hands on my ears, on my pretty new earrings, and he clutched and yanked as hard as he could, and then his face was close to mine and I could feel my ear lobe tear and I started to cry and then his mouth was on my cheek, his teeth digging in, ripping the skin, the skin of my face and my ear, and I screamed and pushed and knocked him away, running for home without looking back.

I had blood on my face, blood on my neck; the earring had been ripped forward all the way through the lobe, leaving me not with a tiny piercing but with a large jagged hole. My mother tried to ask me what happened, tried to wipe off the blood, but I was sobbing and my nose and mouth filled with mucous and I started to hiccup and I couldn't say much except "Todd hurt me."

There was a knock at the door. My mother went to answer it, and I could hear the voice of Todd's mother; she was yelling, and she had Todd with her. I ran to the pantry and hid in the very lowest cupboard and pulled the sliding hollow door shut behind me, cowering in the dark. I could hear Cindy telling my mother the story of what happened; she made Todd pull down his pants to show a red mark from the jump rope. My mother listened and then said, "Well, my kid has her ear ripped half off, and bite marks on her face." My mother didn't sound angry, just stiff and formal, as if this comment was the end of the discussion, the bill is in the mail, good-bye. She was good friends with this woman, whose daughter was my best friend. We went places together, to the zoo, inner tubing, camping on the coast.

After Cindy left, my mother slid the pantry door open. "Come out," she said, and she didn't sound happy.

"Next time," she said, "you have to hit back."

It's easy enough to break the rules when you are too poor to feed your family but not poor enough to receive government benefits, when you're a family living on a boy-man's salary for delivering newspapers or pumping gas or part-time work in the forest.

THE WOMEN IN MY FAMILY HIT BACK. SOMETIMES THEY HIT FIRST. Not usually in a provocative way, not to start a fight—but in the middle of a fight, when the rage over some enormous transgression boiled over. It's easy enough to break the rules when you live not only in poverty, but in the lowest dregs of working poverty, too poor to feed your family but not poor enough to receive government benefits, when you're a family living on a boy-man's salary for delivering newspapers or pumping gas or part-time work in the forest. Often, there would be an argument over something the boy-man bought. A model car, a magazine, tickets to a movie, a special treat—and that money should have gone toward a loaf of bread. They would argue, then scream, and the boy-man would have a shaking tantrum. These men, even the violent ones, were just boys who broke the rules. If a fight started in the car, it usually ended with the man dropped off on the side of the road, kicked out to walk home or bum a ride off a stranger.

But sometimes, someone would raise a hand and hit. Then they would fall on each other, stand back up, fall back down, go waltzing around the room in a macabre dance of violence (but they did not know how to waltz, so perhaps it was a square dance, a do-si-do), while I sat in the crackly green reclining chair and watched Westerns on television.

Nobody hit *me*, not even as a measure of discipline. My cousins were cuffed routinely; someone was always threatening to cut a switch; smacks fell down like rain. But I was absolutely protected within this family, because my mother would not let anyone touch me, and because I was a bleeder. My nosebleeds were frequent and copious—I could soak a towel or fill the sink basin just from riding in a car or reading too long or falling asleep in an awkward position. If I felt sad, I coughed up blood. Growing up, I was usually sick, curled up with a blanket and an infected organ, ear, throat—recuperating perpetually, watching television and reading books. People had fights, they hit each other, and I was never touched.

I saw fights between my Aunt Louisa, the baby of the family, a teenager still with short hair and David Bowie T-shirts, and her husband, my favorite, who drove a VW van and wore purple high-top sneakers with plaid bell-bottoms. His parents had a lake cabin, an impossible luxury, and we used to float around the lake on inner tubes, lazily stroking the murky water, and then climb up the steep stairs to the A-frame cabin where three boys spent summers in a perfect—sitcom-perfect, like *Hazel* or *Father Knows Best*—childhood. Aunt Louisa used the baby's diaper bag to hide their stash of drugs, and I know that when they broke up, someone hit someone else, and my aunt's eardrum was punctured, but it was never clear to me why my now ex-uncle was the bad guy. He always seemed so nice, and my aunt, well, there was the story about the time she wouldn't stop kicking one of her sisters in the car and the car went in a ditch and they ended up pummeling each other in the middle of a busy road.

It was understood, though never discussed, that the habitual, reflexive violence in our family was an expression of strength, that we were not abused but merely querulous. We were the strong ones, the victorious, and the women in the family were to be honored for their ability to fight. The women whispered about the new bride's younger sister, Susie, who had married a man with a moustache and mean eyes. He hit Susie and she just put her hands across her eyes, crying. Susie showed up with bruises on her arms, black eyes, and a big pregnant belly. My mother and her sisters said that if she couldn't protect herself she should leave, or, failing that, kill him; they nodded and agreed that they would never let a man get away with that shit.

When her baby was still in diapers she was pregnant again and she tried to leave, but the man broke down the door and beat Susie up, left her bleeding on the floor, took his son, and disappeared forever.

Some fights were so legendary, discussed so often, it was easy to imagine you had been a witness even if you weren't born yet when the event occurred. My Aunt Signe, my mother's oldest sister, had a wretched husband, the worst kind of bad imaginable. She had a good job as a secretary in the shipyard, and one day in the middle of an argument he swept up all of her work clothes and took them outside. He threw the clothes in their muddy driveway and then drove back and forth over them with his car. When he came back inside he was laughing and he picked up a bottle of wine and raised it to his lips for a drink. She smacked that bottle into his mouth, shattering teeth and glass—bone and blood and glass and wine spilling forward across the kitchen table as he screamed.

One day they had a fight about dog food and he hit her and she grabbed a knife and chased him out of the house. He ran down the driveway and she got in her station wagon and knocked him down and drove over him, grinding him into the mud and gravel, just like he had driven over her beige pantsuits, permanent-press skirts, blouses with ruffled collars.

It didn't kill him; we believed he was too wicked to die. We whispered, "Too bad she didn't use the truck" as he passed through the dining room on his way to torment someone in the living room, hobbling on crutches, stinking of motor oil and whiskey. Of course, my aunt would have gone to prison, which would have been bad, because she was the respectable one, with a nice hairdo and a job in the shipyard, and she was smart and funny.

One bright, sunny day I was driving across the Tacoma Narrows Bridge, Mt. Rainier on the horizon and sailboats far below. I was wearing an electric-blue mini-dress. My hair was long and blond, held back with a chiffon scarf, and my legs were covered with laddered tights, black boots to my knees. I had a boyfriend of rare beauty sitting next to me, and we were driving to Seattle to see a band called Pure Joy.

I reached out to change the radio station and he smacked my hand away. Without pause for thought, my hand curled into a fist and my arm jerked back, up, and with vicious force connected with the face of this pretty boy. Without forethought or planning, without losing control of the car hurtling at fifty miles per hour over a high bridge, I hit him as hard as I could. He held both hands to his face. His voice was muffled and he started to cry. "You broke my nose," he said.

This was neither the first nor the worst of our many fights. After the episode on the bridge, I would like to say, that was the end, the moment, the signifier. But my courage, the purest and most valiant part of me, did not match my wisdom. I tried to break up with him after a while, and I told him we had broken up, but he didn't believe me. More important, I had broken one of the most important rules of those who practice domestic violence: I hit above the neck. The arm that struck the blow would have to pay. After that day on the bridge, every time we fought, he grabbed my wrist, twisted, shoved—shoved my elbow into a wall with a dull thud, or punched the lee of the joint with a sharp pop. On cold mornings or when the season changes, my arm gets numb, and sometimes there is a flash along the nerve that runs between the smallest finger and the elbow, reminding me of those teenage games.

We were in love, and it was a passionate and enormous love, and the dialectic of our family lives (for his mirrored my own) never taught us how to act any differently, to restrain ourselves, to enjoy the quiet things in life. He touched my scars and said that I was beautiful. We were young and reckless and the sex was good and the laughs were fine and it was delightful, addictive, to be alive.

We broke up eventually out of boredom, because we wanted to kiss other people. My teenage love saga ended with a different boy, years later, an honorable boy inevitably corrupted by the reality of life in a hard poor town and the dangers that befall children when their mothers are not vigilant in protecting them, body and soul. This story ends with a 9-mm handgun held at my right temple, as I looked into the eyes of a boy who would never have hit me. This was our contract, we had figured out that much: He would never hit me, nor would I touch him in anger.

But we were both damaged by our short, fast lives and the inescapable events that brought us to this particular clean moment, standing in a shabby white kitchen of a dank basement apartment, dirty dishes on the counter, school papers scattered everywhere.

In a different kind of story he would be portrayed as shaking with rage, flushed with power, blustering and roiling with emotion. But in real life he was steady and determined, the barrel of the gun pressing against my skin an admonition, a benediction; and I neither doubted his intent nor his ability and willingness to act.

He would argue, "But you had a knife," and this is true. I had a good knife, a sharp and lethal knife, pressed to his belly, and knew how to use it. Even if I couldn't survive this fight, I could inflict damage.

I looked at his round young face, pale and freckled, at his brown eyes as he decided exactly when to pull the trigger, and remembered all the other moments of rage, the other fights I had won or lost, and felt a despair deep as any mountain lake. I thought, "This can be the end of all the fighting, it would be so easy." Simply being alive had been such a terrible war of attrition, I had survived by a narrow margin, and I could have chosen to do so many other things with my hard-won victory. I could have traveled, or learned to sing, could have done anything in the world, and I had chosen this boy and this moment. I had used up all of myself and ended up no more than a mile from my childhood home. I was just on the far side of the same forest. The rage emptied out of me and I was calm. "Put it down," I said quietly, and I continued looking into the madness of his eyes until his eyelids fluttered and closed, and he stepped away.

ALL OF THE PEOPLE IN THESE STORIES MANAGED TO GROW UP AND settle down and stay together, and eventually, to stop fighting, and still love each other. Or they chose death. But even with the example of many long marriages, fractious but no longer violent, or the wretched uncle eventually tamed and consigned to a wheelchair, or the honest and simple suicides and murders, I could not or would not move beyond the moment with the gun at my temple. That was the end of a specific relationship, but also the end of my rage. It was the last fight.

I walked away from my lover, my family. I stepped out of the diorama, tore up the placard, walked away from the box that contained the scenes of battle. I moved away and started over with a new identity; with a new family; with scores of friends, chosen carefully.

One of my young friends was confiding in me recently about her problems with her lover, and wanted advice, or at least a little perspective. I shrugged and said, "Maybe you should date someone who had a happy childhood." This is advice I inflicted on myself after the fighting stopped, and ten years of decency has proved worth the effort (and just as exciting). It is not easy, it is in fact harder, to be vulnerable, to be kind.

I'm still attracted to damaged people, the grown-up children of violence, the people who keep secrets and show off lies.

I'm still attracted to damaged people, the grown-up children of violence, the people who keep secrets and show off lies. But I keep them at a certain safe distance, and politely decline to play. I have a strict and repressive code of conduct for myself, and I will not fight, nor debate, nor will I even speak to people who might cause me to fall again, to take that reckless, thoughtless slide down into rage.

Those of us who grew up fighting know one another without telling these stories; we can smell it, maybe, or perhaps see it in the way a hand rests on a table. Maybe we hold our bodies differently; maybe the secret crosses our faces before we even know that we have given it away. I do not consciously try to convey information with my body, but I've never been panhandled or harassed on the street. Nobody has ever asked me out on a date or flirted with me in a social setting. I can walk through a large crowd and people move swiftly out of my way.

In this adult life I have had only two opportunities to fight. The first happened several years ago, on a dark night with no moon or stars, a cold night. I had put my baby into the back of the car, buckled the car seat, and was about to get in when I sensed danger. I turned around and a man had materialized, not near the car, but actually standing within the curve of the door. He reached out with both arms and I pulled back my fist and he saw, through the scrim of light from the car, the expression on my face. He pulled his hands back, held them in front of his face, jumped back a foot, stumbled, and apologized before running away into the darkness.

Another day, a dry autumn day, I arrived home with my children and unlocked the door. The living room looked strange; something was missing, and I could see through a doorway that my study had been searched; clothes I had left stacked on the desk were strewn across the floor, wires pulled out of the wall. Standing in the living room I could see that the back door was still locked. I sent the children back outside. I grabbed the nearest possible weapon, a large metal flashlight, and ran up the stairs. My only thought was to find and hurt the person who had invaded my home, who might have hurt us. It wasn't until I had checked all the closets and stood next to the broken window, the route of entry and escape, that I realized what a foolish choice I had made. My instinct was not to get help, but rather to attack.

This is my meditative discipline: a constant wakeful awareness of danger. My blood contains the secrets, the knowledge of hospital corridors and the threat of injury. I can only offer the most obvious lesson I have learned: that anger feeds rage and rage breeds violence and that people who allow anger to dwell in their bodies and minds perpetuate the cycle. But I'm not didactic about it; I'm not testifying. I don't really care enough to convince anyone to change. Life is complicated, and if I hadn't known how to defend myself, I would not have survived. I just want to keep my small family safe and to stay here, laughing, until it is time to go.

SCHOLARSHIP BABY

LEAH LAKSHMI PIEPZNA-SAMARASINHA

"You got one ticket to ride, kid. Don't blow it."
—my mother

I BLEW IT.

Scholarship baby, ticket-to-ride holder, geto supastar, grassroots intellectual: So much of who I am is about being my mother's exceptional daughter. Is about getting my first scholarship at age eight.

Proposition 21/2 cut taxes and destroyed Massachusetts's public school system, all the teachers under age fifty got fired, and my mama had me in the admissions office of the local one-horse K–12 private school before I could blink. Her voice changed in there, just the way it did when the phone company was on the line. I was so bright and exceptional, so different. She wore her best Filene's Basement and smiled just right. I got in and stayed till I was eighteen, and it worked; I'd rocked my way to three APs and a $25,000 scholarship to NYU. I was the smart kid in big brown plastic glasses and factory-outlet shoes. I was not gonna be a hairdresser on black beauties like my cousins. Maybe we were back in Wormtown 'cause it was the only place my mother could afford a house, but she was gonna keep snapping at me whenever I said "Wuh-stah," and keep buying the best secondhand cars she could afford.

But what happens when you don't grow up to bust outta your hometown into the stars? When you're the one who gets away, but you don't? 'Cause if you fuck up your one chance, that's it. Right?

I'M IN TORONTO, I'M TWENTY-THREE. THERE'S A NATIONAL BORder between me and my family for a reason. And I am not the lawyer or doctor my parents dreamed was going to cement the deal. I'm still on a visitor's visa and can't access the free health care we'd dream about back home. We knew folks who'd drive up to Montreal and scam free prescriptions for Seldane meds from the clinics, but that was before welfare reform, tip lines, and photos on the health cards. I'm sick. I'm in a fucked-up house that has a back yard but is under the power lines and by the tracks. I can't afford rent or food. I'm working under the table. Make no long-distance calls so the phone won't be cut off. Use my eyes and smile and voice to make Immigration like me. I'm passing as a slumming, middle-class college kid who's breezy about the rent to my landlady. I listen to the train chugging by. Walk everywhere. Start eating meat again—for one more dollar, shwarma goes farther than falafel. I don't use social services. Not gonna look good if I get called for that interview. I've got one shot.

"Our generation's screwed," this boy I met on the fifty-dollar Toronto–Montréal van said. "We all grew up thinking nobody was gonna ever make money."

NOBODY'S REALLY RICH IN WORMTOWN. THE ONES WHO THINK they are own used-car lots and outlet-mall stores, but damn, they're doing better than the rest of the town. And of course there are the petty nobility: the folks who go to the Worcester Club, who showed up on some tag-along to the fuckin' *Mayflower*.

The whitest people in the world live in New England. In the New Haven bus station bathroom, on our way to a gig at Yale to do a performance about class for the rich South Asian kids having a conference about it, I see them for the first time in years—the fine-boned blondes who look like Jill on *The Practice*, the ones I grew up closer to, big Irish-Polish faces, big hair, first acid-wash and now booty jeans.

Fumes from Norton, the world's largest manufacturer of ceramic tile, blew over the school. When the wind blew the right way it stank of garbage or burning tar. Every year a teacher got either breast cancer or alopecia, and we got used to watching their hair drop out bit by bit during class. Worcester is the only place I've ever heard of where working-class folks try to afford bottled water and it's 39¢ a gallon, just for the town. The second girl I kissed, who grew up in Leominster (known for the uranium that leaked into the water), found out she had cervical cancer at thirty, during the mandatory pelvic for egg donation—her first health care in ten years. All the downtown was abandoned: Funland, the toy store with the big rotting clown murals that'd gone bust; Union Station, back when working-class cities had department stores and strollable downtowns, now with trees growing up through the roof. Half-cracked parking lot and thirteen-story high-rises with all the windows busted out.

My mom had tried to flee Worcester. She made it partway. All the way to two master's degrees on scholarship, at night, at Anna Maria College and Assumption College, little shit colleges no one had heard of. All the way to getting a Fulbright to Uganda to study then, when the Idi Amin government expelled whites from the country, to London. All the way from being the one girl in her high school class to go to college. Everyone else pregnant, working in the mills, or married. Webster, Massachusetts, in 1956 was a long way from having any respect for nerdy intellectual girls. The only reason she got to go is because a teacher pulled her aside and was shocked that she wasn't college-bound, called up the registrar at Worcester State, and got her in. She worked at Nectarland Ice Cream parlor and in the office at the textile mill while she was in college, made a couple thou a year after she graduated. But she was a teacher.

My mama found herself back in Worcester because class is a hard thing to shake unless you're the strongest and the fastest and jettison everything to survive. And even if you're willing to strip off your family and your history, you might end up like she did—finally married at thirty-two to an exotic Sri Lankan bumming around Europe, who, it turned out, didn't have the university education he claimed on forms. My dad used his "more British than the British" accent and lovely manners to scam his way into a series of midlevel administration jobs, only to be fired mysteriously from each one. They moved back to the States, the economy crashed; they moved back to Worcester, where you could buy a house even if you were broke. It was the place my mom had spent all her life trying to flee.

But she never let me forget that she had almost made it. Halfway. A foot in. Not knowing upper-class people, not liking them, but studying them. Teaching them there is one accent for home and one for being out in the world. Teaching me to be bright and exceptional. I had a job. I was gonna get all that free money, get in to a good school 'cause I was brilliant, and move on up. I was not going to fall. You fall and you get stuck forever, in the pit of nowhere people that don't matter. But we hate the rich kids; they don't know anything real, anything about life. We ride shotgun. It's a mindfuck.

My light brown skin and green eyes are part of what makes me a good case. My mom works that too. I'm not classified as one of the "minority students." It's more like I'm seen by admissions as the kid who is a quarter "something"—a drop for garnish, but not enough to be an "issue."

In classes with the blond, pale WASPs only New England can produce, it's different. It's about being ugly. I was never called "dothead" or "spook," but "ugly": ugly being brown, kinky hair; dark skin; glasses; height; tits and hips and blood in fifth grade; leg and armpit hair thick and curling black. Just ugly. Ugly doesn't look good in eighties discount-barn clothing, powder blues and pinks, acid wash; ugly doesn't look good in big hair, hairspray, and bangs. Ugly is too smart, reads all the time, likes school.

We would drive down 290 to T.J. Maxx, where we would slowly, methodically, go through the whole store. A four-hour job. You look at every piece there 'cause only four will be doable, not trashy looking. The only Brooks Brothers suit on triple discount. Navy blue, black, taupe, nothing too colorful, one pair of outlet shoes. When I'd gone to public school I wore the same shirts from Zayre's or Caldor everyone else wore.

Siobhan, my best friend from grades three to five, and I were the two scholarship kids, the first ones. An experiment. Her mom kept her last name and didn't give a shit. They were French Canadian. Siobhan was dark like me and had her own room in the basement of their tiny tract house out in Quabbin Hills, where every one of the bedrooms had two or three bunk beds for all the new kids who kept coming. Siobhan's room was Foxfire library books, fantasy board games, and the weeds we dried when we were playing out in the backyard—the yard that was acres of weeds and trees.

I remember my mother walking through Cambridge on the Saturday trips we would make every six weeks. The routine never varied. We would hit Urban Outfitters in the morning to look at outfits I could never afford to buy, then Bertolucci's or Uno's for pizza, then one of Cambridge's many bookstores to gorge. One book. We'd look, not buy, but we went every six weeks without fail. I remember walking through all the people who were intellectuals, my mother's dreamy eyes. I remember her stopping outside a fancy boutique window to say, reverently, "The Beaujolais Nouveau has come in," longing. My parents never would be able to afford Boston. Not without admitting they had the money they had and getting housing in a neighborhood—maybe a little poor, brown around the edges or at the heart—that also reflected who they really were.

I ALWAYS IMAGINED I WOULD GO TO HARVARD. WALK THOSE brick sidewalks, go to all those bookstores, be with all the truly smart people. "You have to begin thinking how to sell yourself," the admissions person announced. Cathy and I slouched in our seats. Cathy was Polish. She had wispy blond fine hair permed and banged around her face, skirt a little too tight. A public school kid. After she'd tried to befriend the jock girls and was rebuffed, with a look of resignation she came to sit at our table. She had been popular at her old school, had had a lot of boyfriends. Still did, but also put Sinead pictures up and aggressively clipped Nike ads about motivating young women in sports. We both knew "things to put on applications" were crucial. You start grooming yourself in eighth grade, if not before. You have to be brilliant early or you won't get in the next brilliant level of classes, won't be recommended for things, will not get accepted into good schools.

The track starts in grade school and you can never fall off. Falling off means falling into the pit of normal people, the ones who torment you or the ones like your cousins. Annie and CiCia are cutting hair, dropping out of Framingham State, doing pills and acid and booze and, occasionally, heroin. They are in their mid-thirties and they are not leaving.

Decked out in the finest artsy wear Worcester can offer, they are still trapped—by loyalty, by letting their feelings keep them from getting that A. Doesn't matter if you're fucked up. Get the union card: the degree.

But how the fuck do you get the degree? I thought once I got there it would be easy. The other freaks and me, we would all be there. But working-class equals unenlightened, dumb, abused, stuck. Right?

It takes a middle-class life to believe you can write for a living. It takes parents who will pay your rent, bail you out, buy you nice consumer gear and electronics, and make sure you have groceries, so you can score those connections. My mother tried to give that to me, but she didn't know quite how. There was a lot of magical thinking going on. You go there and if you're good, you get it! If you can't figure it out, well, "I dunno, Leah, how do you expect me to know?" She was small and shabby, shy and fierce. I could see her holes at the end; they hurt. She was not shining and clean and she could not hold on to her pride. She spent too much time trying to hide what she was. Oh, what a strange world she had let me believe in.

I want to be an activist. How murderously she looked at me when I said that. But she wasn't quite sure I was wrong, either. My career should be something I loved, something that allowed me to always have health insurance, something that was creative, something that was secure. Plant genetics or non-profit, maybe; anyway, something with letters after my name.

Grad school? Financial aid was taken away in the nineties, no more free money.

It makes me think a lot about class and activism and how they got me here. I think about the folks who are all creamy over their fantastic activist jobs and the weird promise of being well paid for the *revolution*. I think about how my mother raised me totally on the myth that I would be the one to get away, that I would scholarship my way outta town and go to Harvard and become a plant geneticist or something, that working-class ticket to ride of "you will never have to hustle again." And at the same time, saying and modeling the view that the system's fucked, everything's fucked, it's not what it says it is, any of it, so find a safe niche and hide until you can retire. Don't believe in the possibility of more 'cause you'll just get screwed.

It's a class thing. She knew that the rich kids' social justice movements would just overwork and underpay her. And she was right. At the same time, she was so focused on passing as "money" that she couldn't talk about any of this shit up front. I didn't wanna be cynical like that. Her eyes would narrow, she'd get so mad when I'd tell her I was gonna get some great activist job. And she was right, too. Kind of.

I ran away 'cause I was an incest orphan and was broke and undocumented. But I ran to the crack of twenty-dollars-an-hour part-time social justice jobs in a country that's still a welfare state. (I had no idea such things existed. Get paid fourteen dollars an hour doing feminist anti-oppressive anti-psychiatry counseling at a women's center with paid breaks and sick days? *Dawg.*)

And since I hustled in on a useless degree meant for girls with more privilege than me, I do better than the other assholes. I help folks make it through the maze 'cause I was in it. I give out phone numbers for free counseling and rent banks like crack, like candy. I give a shit. And I am still part of a social control system where reporting to Children's Aid is mandatory, where being too much of a "client" ain't cool, unless you want to be a "Look! I made it too!" street-kid-to-social-work-lady success story. The nonprofit activist heaven where "underprivileged" kids rise through our anti-oppression gospel, get jobs, are saved. Often, unfortunately, they cannot become just like us, and stay "clients." A different species. One the jobs depend on. How do "activists" who don't have a daddy to fund them subsidize our way through life without falling into wage-slaving, working at shit that sucks up our lives? Is it possible to create enough nonprofit jobs to employ all the "at-risk youth" in the world? And is this really as far as we want to go?

That's my way. Beauty out of nothing.
Twenty dollars in the drawer, friends,
and prayer for the hard times.

I want to tell my mom that there are other options, between beauty and assimilation, failing and being shit. That life don't give us a lot of choices, but the choices are bigger than she thought. Not 'cause this is a land of opportunity, but because this is a land of hustle, chaos, and a free market that constantly mutates what it allows. I'll get my words in print, but I won't always use the right accent to stay there.

We used to steal bricks out of construction sites when I was a kid. Go out at night and load them up. We made over that back yard to look like something nice, something in *Family Circle*. I want to tell her: That's my way. Beauty out of nothing, Ma, with a little more than you had. Twenty dollars in the drawer, friends, and prayer for the hard times. We need a lot of tickets to ride, a lot of chances. I didn't make it like you thought, but I made it another way. And I'm still exceptional, along with all the others. Beauty and brilliance right here.

SOMETHING FROM NOTHING

SHAWNA KENNEY

NOTHING.

My sister swears she doesn't remember a single thing about our childhood. I remember specific details of every photo I see of us, when it was taken and exactly how I felt posing. I have one of me on my second birthday, sitting next to her with my hand on her baby carrier. I'd plopped down beside her on Grandpa's round rag rug seconds before the shot, feeling quite big-sisterly, like I knew it was forever my job to "betect" her, this little being, from everything.

There is one of us a couple of years later taking a bath, me smiling coquettishly at the camera, her looking down into the Mr. Bubble–foam, the two of us safe together in the belly of the white ceramic lion-pawed tub-beast. Minutes later Mom would lift us out individually, drying and powdering our little bodies with undivided attention. This was well before we knew the word "project" could mean anything other than something you made with paste and construction paper, or that our kingdom was a place people whispered about and where some cab drivers refused to go. It was in these unhurried moments I felt most loved.

For fun we bounced between playing "Kathy and Judy"—our favorite game of "betending" to be coffee-slurping, fake-cigarette-smoking, agitated moms with always absent good-for-nothing husbands to complain about—and playing school, fooling around with clay or playing freeze-tag with the neighborhood kids. I don't tell too many people about the game of "barbecue" I instigated, which involved everyone getting a stick, poking at a pile of old dog poop as if it were meat on a grill, and voilà—a "barbecue." The game usually ended with us chasing each other around, screaming, "*Gonna put it on youuuuuuu!*" We had no back yard and had never been to a real barbecue, but Barbecue was our game—a secret the adults could know nothing about. Thanks to my dad's sense of adventure, we also enjoyed weekend fishing, day trips to local parks, and my favorite—visits to whatever garage he was working at to play "mechanic's assistant." Both my sister and I had learned the difference between a wrench and a hammer by age four, and a flathead versus Phillips screwdriver by five. I learned to keep this quiet after one time in second grade when, playing hangman, the kids couldn't figure out my word. I'll never forget their looks of suspicion and disgust when I revealed it to be "crankshaft." I didn't know exactly what it was, but I knew how to spell it.

Later we learned that Dad made lopsided, too-loose pigtails when Mom had to be at work early. We learned daddies were strong. I remember my dad lying prostrate with arms outstretched, each of us standing stick-straight in the palm of his hand while he lifted us up into the air. We were wide-eyed and giggly at his Superman-like strength. One year for Christmas, Santa Claus brought us a child-sized wooden table with four matching chairs, from then on referred to as "the little table." Dad bought Mom a Mr. Coffee, which started an argument about them not being able to afford such a luxury. She demanded that he return it. Words got louder and louder, and my sister and I scooted into the small space under the couch like we did during thunderstorms. The argument ended with our dad throwing one of the new little chairs against the wall, sticks of wooden shrapnel flying everywhere. He brought the coffeemaker back; my parents kissed and made up; but the "little table" remained a three-seater, perfect for me, my sis, and one doll-baby, but forever a reminder of how Superman could change into the Hulk in a heartbeat.

I was in third grade when I noticed another weakness in my father—what an obstacle words were for him. Studying for a spelling test, I asked him to help, instead of my mom. I took the list and asked him to spell "elephant." He used an "f." I'll never know if he was pulling my leg, but later when I told my mom in private horror, she laughed and agreed that Dad was "an awful speller." From then on I noticed that he always did the bills, while Mom was "the letter-writer." Though only educated to the tenth grade herself, she was always writing a letter to the editor about some injustice or preparing job bids for my father.

My favorite piece in our old photo albums is a yellowed newspaper clipping of my father and his two brothers in Navy uniforms, with the caption "Kenney Boys Home for Christmas." It was an allowance made during the war thanks to my mom's letter-writing campaign to the governor of New York and the president, based on some law forbidding all male members of a family to be away at war at the same time. My father's handwriting still looks like my childhood scrawls—tiny, illegible hills and valleys of inky, incomplete letters smashed together, perhaps to hide his bad spelling.

Our white kitchen floors, which smelled of bleach, were "clean enough to eat off of," my mom always said, and sometimes we did, when we had a full house. I remember thinking that elbow macaroni with tomatoes thrown in was food fit for kings, and that Mom making Popsicles with Kool-Aid in ice-cube trays was a damn genius summer treat. I liked picking at the peeling corners of our cracked linoleum, but my mom yelled at me to stop if she saw me, saying, "That bastard landlord is supposed to fix that soon." I thought "bastard" was a term of endearment back then, since Gramps sometimes half-yelled, half-laughed, "Get down off the countertops, ya bastards!" while we raided his cupboards with our cousins. We played for hours with the neighborhood kids, all equals in the red brick jungle and patches of grass. The same brick jungle my mom grew up in. Stella, the deaf lady next door who sometimes yelled out the window at us in her low nasal voice for "being too rough," used to yell at her, too.

Shane Matzeo had no dad, but he had Monopoly-like plastic money to buy stuff with at the corner store. I wanted it, too, but my mom got mad when I asked. "That's welfare. Your parents work," she said. Shane was my age and sometimes my unofficial boyfriend. We touched the tips of our tongues together on the front step once, because he said that's how you kiss. We giggled afterward and promised not to tell. He had a little sister named Rachel, same age as mine, and we four played together a lot. Once, when playing Monster, Shane was "it" and chased my sister through his house until she put her arm through the glass front door. We all went to the hospital and she got fifteen stitches, so we weren't allowed to play with the Matzeo kids for awhile.

Jason Spanelli spent summers and holidays with his grandparents down the street, not exactly in the housing development, but close enough to play with us. He was a fat kid with a crush on my sister. The neighborhood whispered about his grandparents being "family," because they had a new car every other week and always paid for everything in cash. Their house was a hangout for his whole extended family, and they always offered you food the minute you stepped through the door. "Sausage and peppers? Some lasagna, Honey? Did you eat?" his grandma would say, coming at you with full steaming plates. Even if you told her you had, she made you have a piece of cake or a "no-thank-you" helping. Mom said she didn't care if they were mafia—"They're still good people," she said. "They brought us food and gave me rides everywhere when I was pregnant with you and your dad was overseas, and I'll never forget that." Plus, they were Catholic and went to our church, so she liked that, too. We were always allowed to play with Jason.

Mindy had more Barbies than anyone, because she had a sister who was fifteen years older who passed down all her

Barbies and Barbie clothes. She also had the Dream Machine, Dream House, Corvette, an Easy-Bake Oven, It's Sew Easy, the Snoopy Sno-Cone Machine, Shrinky Dinks, and that Operation game. Her toys were powerful currency when she didn't get her way. "*Welllllll*, if I can't be teacher today, you can't borrow my Barbie disco outfit overnight," she'd say, and eventually someone would give in, usually my sister. Mindy's things were all she had going for her.

Gramps lived next door with Grandma, who was sent away to the funny farm for "nerves" before I was born. I don't know what made her so nervous, but it had something to do with the hysterectomy she had after having my uncle Chuckie, who "wasn't quite right in the head," according to most people. Since then Grandma hadn't been right either, and she had been in and out of this funny farm, which seemed like a great place because when she came home for holidays she brought lots of mosaic ashtrays and other art projects she'd made. She never talked much, just sat chain-smoking calmly with her legs crossed all ladylike, but the top leg or foot was always bouncing up and down furiously. I think this was the "nerves." One time she drank almost a whole bottle of beer my dad had set down, and everyone freaked out. "Frances, you know better! It'll kill you with your medicine!" my grandpa screamed. She laughed and kept on bouncing that leg.

Our cousins lived in a real house down the street—seven kids in one family, so there was always someone to play with there: Bobby, Greggy, Shelly, Sherry, Cindy, Butchie, Mikey. In that order. My uncle Butch died in a car accident when Cindy and I were six. I sat in the car with my dad during the funeral.

It was raining hard and I wanted to go up to the grave site with my mom and cousins, but I was too young. I did get to go to the wake, where there was lots of food and crying and laughing, old ladies I didn't know kissing and hugging on me and my sister. Uncle Butch and his friend had been driving drunk, too fast. Partying, as usual. He wouldn't have wanted anyone crying, everyone said. This was the day I learned the word "decapitated."

We never did end up at that mysterious "poorhouse" Gramps was always talking about. We were spared the labels of "homeless," or worse, "stinky." Even if we were wearing our cousins' hand-me-downs, one weekend being dragged to the St. Vincent de Paul Society to serve soup or hand over our own hand-me-downs was enough to prove that there were people worse off than us, and that they didn't all live in China.

One year I did some readings in the United Kingdom. I stayed at the British Library one whole day, giddy with the idea of me looking at the original manuscripts of *Rikki-Tikki-Tavi, Finnegans Wake, Jane Eyre*. My first reading was in Chatham, east of London. I took the train out to Basildon and a sales rep took me around to four chain bookstores to sign stock. The bookstore people were really nice. South-By-Sea looks like the British version of Coney Island, a town next to a run-down amusement park on the water. I was walking around and thinking how lucky little ol' me was to be there, thinking how I'm from nowhere, never thought I'd go anywhere, how people from nowhere sometimes get stuck and sometimes break out, when I stumbled on a cobblestone and skinned my knee. I ripped my cute new black striped tights, and later, while gently pulling them out of the blood and rocks embedded in my leg, the words of my parents crept into my head—"Can't have nothin'!"—a phrase sputtered whenever anything of meaning or value was destroyed, as though we were destined to never have anything "nice."

These words were most often blurted when someone else in our neighborhood stole or ruined something of ours. Later, when we moved from the projects, the phrase was uttered less and less often. My parents must have known it would be hard to "have anything" living among others who had nothing. Dog eat dog. Poor stealing from the poor. It happened sometimes, and it did seem especially cruel and unexpected. You expected the poor to steal from the rich, the rich to tax or exploit the poor, the rich to steal from one another (or else how would they be rich?), but people with nothing taking a little something from other people with nothing? Insulting. Painful. Just wrong.

MY SISTER MIGHT NOT REMEMBER "CAN'T HAVE NOTHIN'," BUT she remembers the feeling. She has a new condo, which she can't wait to show me, she says. She swipes a card and we walk through an Italian-marbled lobby, down soft, salmon-colored carpeting, and then are whisked up in silent, jetlike elevators. We walk through a winding maze of halls, passing no one. She unlocks the door and waves me in to a catalog-perfect, neat-as-a-pin, color-coordinated living room. There are gray marble kitchen countertops, fake flowers in a slender vase on a glass-topped table in the breakfast nook, perfectly arranged photos of perfectly smiling people on a shelf. There's an old one of me. Price stickers are still on the backs of some of the frames. The bedroom is immaculate. Headboard matches the dresser, big fluffy pillows on top of a big down comforter. Not a shoe peeks out from under the bed. Not a hint of make-up lies around the bathroom sink. Everything is as it should be.

She tells you the cost of everything because she wants you to know she can have it.

It's like a display model, like one of the many little homes with minimal furniture and fake televisions we looked at when our parents went house-shopping in our teens. It looks like no one lives there until she pulls out four pairs of black pants she just bought. She pulls them from a closet full of similar black pants. But these are designer, she tells me. They still have the tags on them. They were expensive but she got them for a good deal, she says. She just paid $500 to have her hair straightened. She tells you the cost of everything because she wants you to know she can have it. In her mind, she has everything. I used to hate her for wanting it.

The only questions she and my parents ask me these days seem to be about things I've bought or can't afford to buy. Are you ever going to be able to buy a house? Don't you need a new car? Do you have health insurance yet? I think they think I have nothing.

I still can't believe my sister doesn't remember anything about the old days. She is in all of my mental snapshots, and when I dig them up, I feel the unintentional camaraderie of poverty, the little pieces of kindness in humanity when conditions weren't ideal. It's my definition of community. I remember it all, enough to write it down, so I know I do have something.

PASSING AS PRIVILEGED

LILLY DANCYGER

I WAS AT A NETWORKING EVENT A COUPLE OF MONTHS AGO, TALKING TO A few other young New York City journalists. As it often does, the conversation drifted into politics—how divided our country is, the importance of hearing opinions that challenge our own, and the responsibility of the media to offer varied perspectives.

"The problem is that you have all of these privileged millennials in New York writing news from inside the bubble!" one member of our group said with a laugh, gesturing around the circle we stood in.

I nodded along. He was right, that is a problem. It's true that the media, especially New York-based online media, is full of twenty-somethings whose parents could afford to send them to expensive schools, to support them through summer internships, and to help out with their rent during those difficult first few years, when journalists make pennies compared to college graduates in other industries.

It's a deeply flawed system that makes it almost impossible for poor or working-class people to work as reporters, writers, or editors—the gatekeepers who decide which topics are worth discussing in newspapers, magazines, and books.

Then I realized he was referring to us—the people in the conversation—as the privileged millennials.

Including me.

I suppose it shouldn't have come as such a shock that my background wasn't immediately readable to these people I'd just met. I was appropriately dressed for the event, I knew the jargon and the talking points, I blended in. What they didn't know is that I'm a high school dropout who was raised by a single mother—a recovering heroin addict with debilitating PTSD who was only able to keep a roof over our heads and food in the fridge with the help of multiple government assistance programs.

When I was a teenager, my "bedroom" was a loft bed above the kitchen of our studio apartment, where my mother slept on the pull-out couch. I got my first waitressing job when I was fifteen, moved out at sixteen, and have been financially independent since.

As I awkwardly wiped condensation from my plastic cup of wine onto my dress slacks, it occurred to me that I'd done such a good job of making something of myself that I'd made my past invisible. The system is stacked against poor kids breaking into the competitive world of journalism, but I did it anyway, and now my peers see my graduate degree from Columbia and my magazine job, and they assume that I must have had help, like they did—that someone paid my rent, at some point. I pass as one of them.

THE FACT THAT I PASS IS, IN ITS OWN RIGHT, A TYPE OF PRIVILEGE—one that's intertwined with my other privileges as an able-bodied white woman. I can choose to show my societal disadvantages or hide them at will, a luxury Black Americans don't have, a luxury many disabled Americans don't have. And my education and employment, no matter how much I had to scrape and scam and fight for them, provide me undeniable advantages over people with backgrounds similar to mine who weren't able to make it out, whether because they were discriminated against by admissions offices or hiring managers, or because they had to skip college to work a menial job and help support their family, or any other reason.

Now that I've made it this far, I can't deny the privileges I have today. But I also can't—and won't—hide where I came from.

My mother joked once that she had actually helped me pay for college by being so poor that I qualified for the maximum amount of federal financial aid. I could barely fake a smile as I thought about how hard it had been to get that financial aid when I couldn't prove my mother's income because she hadn't filed taxes for the last five years. I'd had to bring in copies of her disability and social security checks—her only income—to prove I wasn't getting any money from her.

Once, when a professor gave an especially short turnaround time for a homework assignment, I approached him after class, asking for more time. I had to work that night, I explained. He told me I needed to make my schoolwork a priority. I agreed. It wasn't worth explaining that I'd have a really hard time doing any schoolwork at all if I didn't have a place to live because I didn't pay my rent. I remembered that moment, and my mother's joke landed with a particularly loud thud.

I took an unpaid summer internship—commonly accepted as an unfair prerequisite to a good job as a writer, but I still bartended at night. I often went straight from my fancy magazine office to the dive bar downtown; dressing for both was an art form I perfected: skinny jeans with a grungy bar tank top hidden underneath a stylish blouse, with red lipstick and black eyeliner stashed in my purse to be applied on the subway. I wondered if any of my classmates had to worry about the absurdity of working full time for free, if they had to go from work to work.

Now I pass. I've made it. So why do I feel so queasy? Why did I have the urge to defend myself at that networking event, to tell the people around me, "I'm not one of you!"

> The usual narrative about the scrappy working-class kid who pulls herself up is that she's supposed to be embarrassed about where she comes from. I don't feel ashamed of my history, I feel ashamed of letting it be erased.

The usual narrative about the scrappy working-class kid who pulls herself up is that she's supposed to be embarrassed about where she comes from. She's supposed to work hard to keep up the illusion, to convince her peers that she, too, went to sleepaway summer camps and lived in college dorms. When she passes, she has succeeded.

But I don't want to blend in. I'm proud of how hard I've worked. I'm proud of the fact that I've never treated waitstaff or security guards or bus drivers like they're not there, that I relate to them more than I do to most of my peers. I'm proud of the fact that I dropped out of high school, and not just because I still managed to go on to get an Ivy League graduate degree, but because I knew what was best for me at the age of just fourteen, and I had the courage to do it.

I don't feel ashamed of my history, I feel ashamed of letting it be erased.

ONE MORNING IN MY SOPHOMORE YEAR OF COLLEGE, I WOKE UP in my loft bed in the tiny apartment I shared with a friend, exhausted from bartending late into the night. I'd only slept a couple of hours, but it was time to get up if I was going to make it to my 10 a.m. Literary Foundations class on time. The sun peeking in my window was blinding, and the smell of French-fry grease and margarita mix clinging to my hair was nauseating.

All I wanted was to turn off my alarm and go back to sleep. I could do it—I could stay in bed, skip class, sleep a little more. Who would care?

Instead, I lay in bed and calculated on my phone exactly how much I was paying per class session. I had scholarships and federal financial aid, but they didn't cover everything. Even with the money I earned bartending, I still had to take out loans to make up the difference. They weighed on my mind as I remembered watching my mother struggle to pay bills and promising myself I'd never agree to pay for anything I couldn't afford. That hadn't exactly worked out, so I figured I had to at least make use of the thing I was going into debt over.

Once I worked out how much money I'd be wasting if I stayed in bed, I dragged myself to class, suddenly seeing my peers with clear eyes—the classmates who didn't want to be there; the ones who skipped class, showed up late, didn't do the homework; who treated college like a four-year party. I knew they weren't paying their own way. If they were, they wouldn't take it for granted.

Once I realized that, I stopped being so jealous and resentful of how easy they had it. I stopped envying their co-signed leases, their rent checks arriving in the mail as if from a giant tooth fairy. They could have all that; I had something they didn't. Call it perspective, work ethic, appreciation, grit. Call it what you will, but I have it, and I won't hide it.

In the moment, at that networking event, I didn't say anything. I did what I had learned to do—blend in and let people assume that I'm one of them. On the subway ride home I was kicking myself for not speaking up, but what would I have said? How could I have told them that I'm not like them without coming off as rude, self-pitying, or both?

Then I remembered that realization I had on that morning when all I wanted to do was skip class: I have something that they don't. I have the perspective that comes with clawing your way into a world that was designed to keep you out.

I don't need to constantly announce to my peers that I'm different from them; I just need to remember that myself. I need to never forget that I have as much in common with the doorman as I do with the fancy women he holds the door open for. I've made it into this world, and now I owe it to the world I came from to hold onto my perspective, my work ethic, my appreciation, my grit, and use my history to be a better writer. To tell truer stories. To speak for the people who were successfully kept out of this world.

ABOUT THE CONTRIBUTORS

Dorothy Allison is the bestselling author of *Bastard Out of Carolina*, *Cavedweller*, and the memoir *Two or Three Things I Know for Sure*. Born in Greenville, South Carolina, she lives in Northern California.

Naomi Begg is a lecturer in English, communication, and creative writing from the Scottish Highlands. She likes yoga, hot tea, the feeling you get when snow is in the air, and death metal. She aims to be a millionaire by the age of fifty and to win a Nobel Prize. Any Nobel Prize will do.

Rachel Ann Brickner is a writer and multimedia storyteller from Pittsburgh. Her writing has appeared in The *Los Angeles Review*, *Joyland*, *PANK*, and elsewhere. Currently, she's at work on her first novel and several projects about debt. You can see more of her work at rachelannbrickner.com.

Once a union organizer at the Lusty Lady Theater in San Francisco, **Siobhan Brooks** is an assistant professor of African-American

Studies. Her writing has been published in *Colonize This! Young Women of Color on Today's Feminism* and *Revolutionary Voices*, and she is the author of *Unequal Desires*.

Chloe Caldwell is the author of the novella *Women* (SF/LD) and the essay collections *I'll Tell You in Person* (Coffee House) and *Legs Get Led Astray* (SF/LD). Her nonfiction has been published in *New York* magazine, *VICE*, Lenny Letter, Longreads, and many anthologies. She teaches creative nonfiction in New York City and lives in Hudson.

Joy Castro is the author of the memoir *The Truth Book: Escaping a Childhood of Abuse Among Jehovah's Witnesses*; two novels, *Hell or High Water* and *Nearer Home*; a book of short stories, *How Winter Began*; and a collection of essays, *Island of Bones*. She is a professor of English and ethnic studies at the University of Nebraska–Lincoln.

Lilly Dancyger is the author of *Hunted: A Memoir of Art and Addiction* and the deputy editor at *Narratively*, where she edits the memoir section. Her essays and articles have appeared in *The Atlantic*, *The Washington Post*, *New York* magazine, *VICE*, and more.

tatiana de la tierra (Villavicencio, Colombia, 1961) is an angry girl who rides horses in the sky and secretly wants to be a songwriter. She is the author of *For the Hard Ones: A Lesbian Phenomenology/Para las duras: Una fenomenología lesbiana* (Calaca/Chibcha Press), a bilingual celebration of lesbianism in poetic prose. She was cofounder and editor of the Latina lesbian magazines *Esto no tiene nombre* (1991–1994) and *Comoción* (1995–1996).

Aya de Leon is an acclaimed writer of prose and poetry and a teacher at the University of California at Berkeley. Her writing has appeared in *Guernica*, *xoJane*, *The Toast*, *Ebony*, *Womans Day*, *Writers Digest*, *Mutha Magazine*, The Good Men Project, KQED Pop, *Bitch Magazine*, *The Feminist Wire*, and more.

Juliana Delgado Lopera is an award-winning writer and oral historian based in San Francisco. The recipient of the 2014 Jackson Literary Award and a finalist of the Clark-Gross Novel Award, she's received fellowships from Brush Creek Foundation of the Arts, Lambda Literary Foundation, and The SF Grotto, and an individual artist grant from the SF Arts Commission and her work has been nominated for a Pushcart Prize. She's the executive director of Radar Productions, a queer literary nonprofit.

Tina Fakhrid-Deen is an educator, activist, writer, performer, and LGBTQ family activist. She is the author of *Let's Get This Straight: The Ultimate Handbook for Youth with LGBTQ Parents*. She lives with her family in Chicago.

Shell Feijo is a former foster kid from Northern California. She lives in Iowa and teaches writing and working-class literature at Kirkwood Community College. Her publications have appeared in *The Fem Literary Magazine*, *Utne*, *Hip Mama*, *The Manifest Station*, and more.

Lis Goldschmidt is a writer, artist, and licensed acupuncturist in San Francisco, where she brings an artist's sensibility to the practice of Chinese medicine.

Ariel Gore is the editor and publisher of the Alternative Press Award–winning magazine *Hip Mama* and the author of eight books.

Terri Griffith is the author of the novel *So Much Better*. Her fiction and criticism have appeared in *Art:21*, *Bloom*, *Suspect Thoughts*, and *Bust*, as well as several anthologies. Since 2006, she has been the literary correspondent and blogger for Bad at Sports, a weekly podcast about contemporary art that focuses on the practices of artists, curators, critics, dealers, and other arts professionals. She teaches writing and literature at the School of the Art Institute of Chicago.

Daisy Hernández is the coeditor with Bushra Rehman of *Colonize This! Young Women of Color on Today's Feminism*. She has written a column for Ms. magazine and reported for *The New York Times*.

Silas Howard is an American director, scriptwriter, and actor. He started as a guitar player in the punk queer band Tribe 8. After creating his first feature film, *By Hook or by Crook*, with Harry Dodge, he went on to get a MFA in directing in UCLA. He began directing episodes during the second season of *Transparent*, making him the show's first trans director.

Shawna Kenney is the author of the award-winning memoir, *I Was a Teenage Dominatrix*. She has written for *Juxtapoz*, *Transworld Skateboarding*, *Slap*, *Tease*, *Alternative Press*, *SG*, *The Underground Guide to Los Angeles*, *While You Were Sleeping*, *Herbivore Magazine*, Epitaph Records, and herself.

Leah Lakshmi Piepzna-Samarasinha is an artist, performer, activist, and author of *Dirty River*, *Bodymap*, *Love Cake*, and *Consensual Genocide*. Her work has appeared in several anthologies, including *Colonize This! Young Women of Color on Today's Feminism*. She is the cofounder of Mangos with Chili, North America's touring queer and trans people of color cabaret.

Bee Lavender is an activist, author, entrepreneur, and social media pioneer. The author of *Lessons in Taxidermy* and editor of the anthologies *Breeder* and *Mamaphonic*, she has written for *The Guardian*, *Salon*, *Catapult*, *Bust*, and *Bitch*, and she has appeared on NPR and BBC Radio. Her work in technology and publishing has been featured in *Wired*, *Fast Company*, *USA Today*, *The Telegraph*, *The Times*, *Time Out*, and *The New Yorker*. She lives in London and New York.

Liz McGlinchey King is a writer living in Los Angeles. She writes about marriage, parenthood, and growing up in working-class Philadelphia. Her essays have appeared in the *Los Angeles Times*, *Mothering* magazine, and the Youshare Project.

Eileen Myles is a poet, novelist, performer, and journalist. Myles's twenty books include *Afterglow*, *Cool for You*, *I Must Be Living Twice*, and *Chelsea Girls*. Myles is the recipient of a Guggenheim Fellowship, an Andy Warhol/Creative Capital Arts Writers grant, four Lambda Book Awards, and the Shelley Prize. The recipient of a Creative Capital grant and the Clark Prize for excellence in art writing, Myles teaches at New York University and Naropa University in Boulder.

Ijeoma Oluo is the author of *So You Want to Talk About Race* and editor-at-large at The Establishment, a media platform run and funded by women. Oluo was named one of the most influential people in Seattle by *Seattle* magazine.

Polyestra is a painter, a poet, and the front woman for the band Polyestra.

Terry Ryan is the author of *The Prize Winner of Defiance, Ohio: How My Mother Raised 10 Kids on 25 Words or Less.*

Wendy Thompson is a writer and filmmaker. Her work has appeared in the anthologies *Restoried Selves* and *Yell-Oh Girls.*

Virgie Tovar is an author, activist, one of the nation's leading experts and lecturers on fat discrimination and body image, and editor of the groundbreaking anthology *Hot & Heavy: Fierce Fat Girls on Life, Love and Fashion*. She is a former plus-size style writer for BuzzFeed, and she has been featured by *The New York Times, Tech Insider, MTV, Al Jazeera, NPR, Yahoo Health*, the *San Francisco Chronicle, Cosmopolitan, Bust* magazine, and more.

Frances Varian is a writer and performer.

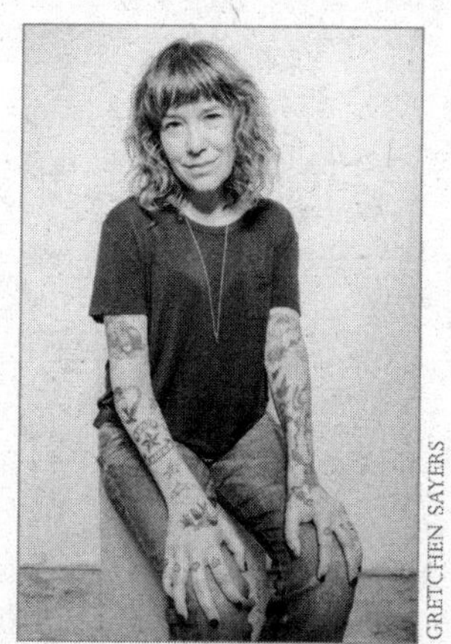

GRETCHEN SAYERS

ABOUT THE EDITOR

Michelle Tea is the author of five memoirs: *The Passionate Mistakes and Intricate Corruption of One Girl in America*, *Valencia*, *The Chelsea Whistle*, *Rent Girl*, and *How to Grow Up*. Her novels include *Mermaid in Chelsea Creek* and *Girl at the Bottom of the Sea*, part of a young-adult fantasy trilogy published by McSweeneys; *Rose of No Man's Land*; *Black Wave*; *Castle on the River Vistula*; and *Modern Tarot*, a tarot how-to and spell book.

Tea is the curator of the Amethyst Editions imprint at Feminist Press. She founded the literary nonprofit RADAR Productions and the international Sister Spit performance tours, and is the former editor of Sister Spit Books, an imprint of City Lights. She created *Mutha Magazine*, an online publication about real-life parenting. Her writing has appeared in *Harper's*, *Cosmopolitan*, *The Believer*, *Marie Clare*, *n+1*, *xoJane*, *California Sunday Magazine*, Buzzfeed and many other print and web publications.